RICHARD V. RO

GOOGLE CLASSROOM FOR

TEACHERS STEP BY STEP GUIDE

A BEGINNER'S GUIDE TO GOOGLE CLASSROOM 2020 - 2021. SCREENSHOTS, TIPS, AND TRICKS FOR THE BEST MODERN TEACHER. INCLUDING PILLS OF MINDSET

© Copyright 2020 - All rights reserved.

TABLE OF CONTENTS

Introduction

What Is Google Classroom?

G oogle Classroom is free of charge web service made by Google for schools. It clarifies paperless structure, dissemination, and marking of homework. Google Classroom's underlying goal is to streamline the file-sharing process between teachers and students. Google Classroom incorporates Google Drive for the production and delivery of tasks, Google Docs, Sheets and Slides for writing, Gmail for collaboration, and Google Calendar for scheduling.

Students can be invited via a special code to enter a college, or imported automatically from a school domain. Every class creates a separate folder in the Drive of the respective individual, where the student can send work for a teacher to assess. IOS applications, which are available for IOS and Android devices, allow users to take images and add to assignments, share files from other phones, and offline access. Teachers can track each student's progress and teachers can return work along with the feedback after grading.

But what distinguishes Google Classroom from the standard Google Drive experience is the interface between teacher and student, developed by Google for the way teachers, and students think and work.

Evolution of Google Classroom

Google Classroom was revealed on 6 May 2014 with a preview available to individual members of Google's G Suite for Education program. It was launched publicly on 12 August 2014. By October 2015, Google reported that certain 10 million students and teachers were using it. Google said about 50 million students and teachers worldwide used Google software from Gmail to Chrome.

In 2015, Google introduced a Classroom API and a website sharing button allowing school administrators and developers to continue their interaction with Google Classroom. In 2015, Google also incorporated Google Calendar into the Classroom for planned assignment dates, field trips, and class speakers.

In 2017, Google enabled Classroom to allow any personal Google users to enter classes without the need for having G Suite or Education account. And, it became possible for any individual Google student to build and teach a course in April of the same year.

In 2018, Google announced a refresh classroom, introducing a classroom section, enhancing the grading interface, allowing teachers to reuse classroom work from other classes, and adding features to organize content by topic. In 2019, Google released 78 new illustrations of the classroom.

For the previous two years, Google has been taking its popular apps and equipping them for classroom use. Although many schools and districts tend to use traditional learning management systems, such as Blackboard, Canvas, Moodle, and Schoology; the eyes of teachers are gradually focusing on Google's Classroom Platform. Most schools are also using the collaboration software suite of Google—Docs, Sheets, and Slides. What Classroom seeks to offer is a way of bringing together these applications and applying new functionality to what teachers and students need. In short, the Classroom is aiming to be a lightweight framework for learning management.

According to the product manager at Google; they spent about a year and a half studying and talking to educators about the app. Apps alert from the guardians and the introduction of multiple teachers to a class were created merely from user feedback.

Does Google Classroom Become An LMS?

Technically, it doesn't. Google Classroom is not a stand-alone program for learning management (LMS), course management (CMS), or student information (SIS) program. That said, Google adds new functions to Google Classroom periodically. For example, in June 2019, Google announced that schools would soon be in a position to synchronize the new grading features of the tool with an existing student information system. As Google continues to add features; it is likely to start looking, becoming more like an LMS to work. Perhaps it's better, for now, to think of the device as a one-stop-shop for class organizing.

Is Google Classroom Free of Cost?

The Google for Education platform is free for schools. Still, there is a paid G Platform Enterprise tier for education, which includes additional features such as advanced video conferencing apps, advanced security, and premium support. Google no longer publishes information about pricing, so you'll want to contact them directly for a quote. Google also offers several free items for authoring tools, web themes, and professional growth, such as Chromebooks, and partners with other companies.

Implementation and integration

Google provides educators and IT Administrators with a range of training choices. These are:

- The Teacher Hub, which provides primary or advanced self-paced Google Classroom preparation and instructor professional development resources.

- Train the Trainer course for people into teaching others.

- Google software Certified Educator and Certified Instructor programs.

- G Suite Certified Administrator program for IT administrators.

Who Is Eligible for Google Classrooms?

The classroom is open to:

- Schools that use G Suite for Education.

- Organizations that use G Suite for non-profits.

- Individuals over the age of 13 with personal Google accounts. Age can vary according to region.

- Both Domains in the G Suite.

Google Classrooms Support Service

Users can access Google Classroom help in the following ways:

- The Help Centre offers information on different topics related to Google Classroom. There is also a troubleshooting section with solutions to common issues.

- There is a software community where users can seek advice from other Google Classroom users and Google Classroom staff.

- Google Classroom also offers regular updates with new features and other software enhancements.

- IT guides for schools' IT administrators also exist.

Can the Classroom be used if G Suite for Education domain includes Gmail disabled?

Yes. Gmail doesn't have to be enabled to utilize the Classroom. If your administrator has not activated Gmail, however, teachers and students do not receive e-mail notifications.

Note: If you set up your mail server and receive information from Drive, you can receive notifications from the Classroom too.

Could the Classroom be used if G Suite for Education domain has been disabled?

No. Classroom collaborates with Drive, Docs, and other tools offered by G Suite for Education to help teachers build and collect assignments, and students submit work online. If you disable Drive: Docs and other services are also disabled. You are not able to add these resources to the research that you allocate to students. Students would also not be able to add these to their jobs. The classroom can still be used, but the collection of features is minimal.

Difference between Google Classroom and Google Assignment

Google Assignments is for organizations using a learning management system (LMS) that want better grading workflows and assignments. It can be utilized as a stand-alone tool and a complement to the LMS, or it can be implemented into the LMS as an interoperability learning tool (LTI) by the school admin. If you are using the Classroom, you already enjoy the best of tasks, including reports on originality.

Accessing Google Classroom from school account and

personal account

Most of the time, the classroom is the same for all users. However, since users of school accounts have access to G Suite for Education, they get further attributes, such as email summaries of student work for guardians and full user account management. G Suite for charity users has the same features as users of G Suite for Education.

Google Classroom for visually impaired people

Google Classroom is a resource designed to help teachers and students interact in the paperless classroom and remain organized there. Visual disability and blindness students can use a screen-reader to access and handle classes and assignments.

Following is the availability for various screen readers:

- **Web:** With any modern browser such as Chrome, Mozilla Firefox, Microsoft, Internet Explorer, or Apple Safari, you may navigate the Classroom using a screen-reader. See the guide on how to set it up in your browser. You can use ChromeVox, for example, with your Chromebook. On Macs, the built-in screen reader, VoiceOver, is used.

- **Mobile:**

  o **Android:** The smartphone app for the Classroom works with TalkBack, a pre-installed screen reader that uses spoken input for interaction.

o **IOS:** The Virtual Classroom app operates on IOS with VoiceOver. For specifics, you might need to see your device's accessibility settings.

Google Classroom API outline

The Classroom API can be used by schools and technology companies to create applications that communicate with Classroom and G Suite for Education and to make Classroom function better to suit their needs. The Classroom API is an API created by Google. That means non-Google companies will benefit from the resources and infrastructure that Google provides.

To use the Classroom API, developers must adhere to the Terms of Service of the Classroom API. Many programs cannot use Classroom data for marketing purposes. Third-party developers and administrators may use the Classroom API. Teachers and students must approve third-party apps. Utilizing the Classroom API, you can do many of the things that teachers and students can do programmatically through the Classroom UI. For example, you can synchronize with the student information systems, display all the classes taught in an area, and control the coursework.

Non-Google services can use the Classroom API to incorporate Classroom features. For example, an app may allow a teacher to copy and reuse a Google Classroom class, rather than re-create the level and re-add every student. Applications may also display, build, and change Classroom work programmatically, add materials to work, turn students' work in, and return grades to the Classroom.

The software must request authorization from the Classroom user before software or service can access Classroom data. The app asks for the individual permissions it requires (such as a username, email address, or photo profile), and the user may approve or reject the request made by the service. The Classroom API uses a popular Internet standard named OAuth to authorize access.

As an administrator of the G Suite for Education, you monitor how the data is exchanged within a domain. You can decide which teachers and students in your area can allow services to access their Classroom data in the Google Admin Console. By organizational unit; you can customize the access. You can also monitor the services that have been given access to a user's account in your jurisdiction in the Admin console, and you may revoke permissions if required.

The different tasks that the Classroom API can accomplish depend on what position a user has in a class. A user can be a student, instructor, or administrator just as in the Classroom UI. Teachers and students should accept applications from third parties and report misconduct.

When the consumer is a (n):

- **Student:** The API can view the course information and teachers for that course.

- **Teacher:** The API can build, display, or remove their classes, show, attach, or remove students and additional teachers from their classes, as well as view and return research, build assignments and topics, and set grades in their classes.

- **Administrator:** The Classroom API can organize, view, or delete any class in their G Suite for Education domain. It can attach or delete students and teachers in their area in all the classes. It also looks at the work and topics in all of the classes in their domain.

There are many explanations for why Google Classrooms are being used for more and more classrooms. The technology is being implemented all around the world, including the US schools and districts through the 1:1 laptop initiative. The initiative features a learning laptop for every pupil. Chromebooks are often chosen because of their affordability and intuitive interface. They are easily integrated with the complete suite of Google apps that includes the Classroom.

CHAPTER 1:

The Modern Teacher

With many online assets, the era can assist improve coaching. Teachers can make use of one-of-a-kind applications or confided in online belongings to develop the customary strategies for coaching and to hold understudies more and more locked in. Virtual exercise plans, comparing programming, and on-line appraisals can help instructors with sparing an exceptional deal time. This sizeable time can be applied for operating with understudies who're fighting. Also, having virtual mastering situations in faculties improves cooperation and statistics sharing between instructors.

Run a Virtual Field Trip

If a place is a long way off due to calculated issues, you may mimic a digital outing by shopping a Google Cardboard for under $15.

There are applications you could use to investigate popular structures, for example, the Empire State Building, and ordinary wonders, for example, the Great Barrier Reef.

You may additionally ask: "By what approach will this interface with gaining knowledge of objective?" You could go to an out of doors milestone, preserving a fake dialogue in that nation's language, or view the region itself from a geographic point of view.

This manner can consist of any other, drawing in factor on your sporting activities.

Review Field Trips Virtually

Likewise, you could utilize Google Earth to investigate areas before clearly traveling them.

Suppose your class is about to visit the Zoo. Discover the area, going through it using Street View to look, which displays provoke the maximum understudy curiosity. You can swiftly have a look at what they're anticipating, boosting fervor tiers for the excursion.

Mainstream area trip goals will likewise have web sites loaded up with visual media you can use to supplement the review.

Everything vital is a gadget related to a projector or full-size display screen.

Calm a Noisy Classroom

To make it less challenging to present sporting activities and introductions, make use of a device that tracks, and indicates school room clamor.

For instance, Too Noisy is an exact commotion meter. You'll probably locate that—without letting students know—understudies will emerge as tranquil while the meter spikes.

This way implies a massive portion of them won't be as troublesome while you give an exercise or run a loose work action. They may also even shush one another.

Like this, you'll have a less difficult time introducing content material.

Use Videos for Mini-Lessons

You can guide your exercise designs employing making use of recordings as independent evaluations for specific subjects.

Additionally, reachable as aptitude audits and critiques, numerous web sites have instructor-made video content material. TeacherTube is a case of education just shape of YouTube, protecting center college subjects.

You can scan for a specific topic or peruse by way of class, unexpectedly finding popular recordings. For instance, scanning for "center school variable based totally math" will stack a results web page containing study publications, particular exercises, and test surveys.

This simple approach to utilize technology in the classroom provides a sight and sound component for your sporting events, which could adequately reverberate with visible rookies.

Research has indicated that the usage of enlivened recordings can decidedly affect a youngster's advancement in a few fitness regions such as memory, imagination, primary reasoning, and important thinking.

Co-Ordinate Live Video

You don't want to confine yourself to pre-recorded recordings, as conferencing technology can permit topic experts to convey physical activities.

Regardless of whether it's a contact from some other school or a prepared trainer you connect to, bringing a consultant into your classroom will open your understudies to new thoughts and can help your remaining challenge at hand.

You can include the man or woman as touch on Skype or Google Hangouts; conveying the exercising through this system. Skype even has a rundown of tourist speakers who will intentionally talk approximately their topics of aptitude.

Pose your understudies to devise inquiries, helping them appreciate— and fulling takes a hobby in—this cutting area tackles traditional physical games.

Play Podcasts

Playing massive virtual recordings can beautify your physical games, yet connect with sound-associated newcomers and go about as a learning station.

Made with the aid of bunches extending from media mammoths to traditional individuals active approximately a particular subject; you can find out digital broadcasts which are:

- Meetings with the writer of an e-book your understudies are perusing

- Exercises approximately examining techniques and techniques

- Investigations of an academic plan related subject

- Talks from educators

For a secondary school direction, you might need to shape a mission that allows understudies to make and play their webcasts.

This way is possibly the most effortless approach to utilize technology in your study room—you certainly need a device with a stable audio system.

Add Multimedia Elements to Presentations

Though slideshow introductions made up of content material can withdraw understudies, ones with sight and sound additives can correctly hold their attention by fluctuating substance conveyance.

When relevant, try to include:

- Pictures

- Charts

- Pictographs

- Digital recording cuts

- Audio cues

- Short video exercises

- News, film and TV application cuts

You don't need to search the Internet to find out large charts and pictographs—you can make them yourself. There are loose on-line devices that find a manner to enter information, other marks, and adjust your plan.

Almost certainly, slideshow introductions as of now have an impact on your sporting events, and such as unique sorts of media can make them all the extra charming.

Send Adaptive Content

If each considered one of your understudies has a mobile telephone and is always on it, why now not utilize the circumstance to, in addition, your potential advantage with the aid of conveying content material through the telephones?

There are versatile getting to know packages that understudies can access through tablets and cell phones.

For instance, ClassK12 offers sentence structure exercises as much as sixth grade Common Core gauges. It's produced from versatile programs that understudies can download onto their gadgets. As a teacher, you may make virtual classrooms, carry assignments, and run reports.

Conveying appropriate substances through such projects may also appear difficult, yet the procedure is typically natural and robotized.

Offer an Online Class Calendar

To hold understudies knowledgeable concerning the substance, they'll be coping with, make, and offer a class schedule that subtleties exercises and capabilities large dates.

You can utilize software, for example, Google Calendar, messaging your schedule's hyperlink on your understudies or their folks.

This manner maintains them educated, yet causes you to continue to be sorted out—you'll rapidly check whether or not you've set an excessive wide variety of due dates in a quick period. Furthermore, by retaining understudies on the up and up; you'll help them with coming arranged for every class.

CHAPTER 2:

Pills of Mindset

oogle Classroom was built for both the educator and the learner in mind. It isn't only the teachers who can do so many things with Google Classroom, but students can also harness the full capabilities of this application. The student's reaction to Google Classroom is whenever the teacher, who is the main Manager of the Classroom, uploads content in the Classroom.

Here are some of the various things that students can do with Google Classroom:

- **Change Ownership:** When you turn in an assignment, the teacher becomes the owner of your document. You are no longer the owner, and therefore you are unable to edit the text. Turned in the wrong assignment? Simply click on the 'Unsubmitted' button. You would need to refresh Google Classroom once you un-submit so that you can resend a new document.

- **Assignment listings:** Students can find a list of all the assignments created by teachers by clicking on the menu icon located at the top left-hand corner of Google Classroom. Practically all assignments that have not been archived can be viewed in this list.

- **Utilize the Mobile App for easier access:** We know students are always on their mobile phones. One of the best ways to get notified if you have a new assignment is through the Google Classroom's mobile app. The mobile app can be downloaded and installed from the Playstore or iTunes. The app allows students to view their assignments and submit their work directly from the app. This mainly works when students are requested to submit real-life samples, or a video or a combination of photos. All they need to do is take pictures of their samples or their solutions and then upload it to the Google Classroom.

- **No worries if you haven't clicked on save:** Encourage your students to use Google Docs to do their assignments. If you have given work that requires them to write reports, write a story, or anything that requires their use of a Word document, use Google Docs because it saves edits automatically. This eliminates your student's excuses for not being able to complete their homework because they did not save it. Also, it just makes things easier when you are so engrossed with completing your work, you forget to save; Google Docs does it for you.

- **Sharing isn't the same thing as turning in:** When a student clicks open an assignment to hand in their assignment; they need to click on TURN IN. Sharing an assignment to the Google Classroom is not the same thing as turning in your completed work. Make sure you click on TURN IN to submit your assignment in due time.

- **You will not lose assignments:** Unless you delete it. Any documents you upload to your Google Classroom is only seen between you and the teacher. Any assignments you upload to your Google Drive will be seen on the teachers' Google Drive as well. Your Google Drive is the storage system for Google Classroom and it works the same way for both the teacher as well as the students.

- **Due Dates:** You'd have a harder time explaining to your teacher why you have not submitted your assignment especially since the due dates are continuously shown on an assignment. Assignments that are not due yet are indicated on the class tile on the home page as well as the left of the page late assignments have a particular folder, where the teacher can accurately see the assignments listing from the menu icon on the upper left of the page.

- **Returning an Assignment:** Students working on a Google Document can return at any time to the file that they are working on. Get back to the assignment stream and click on Open and it will take you to a link to the documents that you have on Google Drive. Click on the document and get back right into it. You can also access this file directly from your personal Google Drive. It is the same way you click on any document on your desktop to work on it again. Plus, the side is Google Docs autosaved.

- **Communicating with teachers:** It's either you communicate publicly on Google Classrooms for the entire class to see, or you communicate privately. Communicating privately helps a lot especially for students who are shy and prefer to speak to the teacher directly without the involvement of other classmates. It also helps the teacher to speak privately to address a student's issue on an assignment without making them feel inadequate or that they have not done well.

- **Commenting on Assignments:** Comments on an assignment are viewable by your classmates on Google Classroom when it is made on any assignments uploaded to the app. Students just need to click on 'Add Comments' under an assignment. If students would like to communicate in private, with you, they can leave it on the assignment submission page. Within a specific document, you can use the File Menu and click on 'Email collaborators' to message or link a document to the teacher.

- **Add Additional files to an assignment:** Students and teachers can both add additional files to an assignment. For students, they can add in files that did not come together with a template the teacher gave. You can click on ADD additional files on the assignment submission page again. Links from websites can also be added. Additional files help in the attempt to provide a wholesome blended learning approach in schools because you can add files of different formats and types.

CHAPTER 3:

Benefits of Google Classroom

As a free online learning system, Google Classroom brings various advantages for students and teachers alike. Here are a few of the key reasons that teachers would try it out for.

Ten reasons teachers should try it out here.

Accessibility

Google Classroom is accessible from any desktop, or with any mobile device, irrespective of software, through Google Chrome.

Both data exchanged by students and teachers are kept in a Google Drive Classroom archive.

The Classroom is open to users everywhere. Students should no doubt be talking about faulty computers or hungry pets.

Exposure

The classroom gives students exposure to an online learning system. Most College and University programs also allow applicants to take part in at least one online class. Exposure at Google Classroom will help students switch to other learning management programs that are common in higher education.

Paperless

Teachers and students will not have to shift excessive amounts of paper as the Classroom is completely paperless. As teachers submit classroom tasks and tests; they are enabled to move concurrently.

Students can complete tasks and assessments straight from the Classroom, and may also hold their job to Travel. Students may have recourse to missed assignments related to absences and will often have certain resources that are possibly needed.

Time Saver

A great time-saver is a classroom. With all the resources saving at one place and getting access to the Classroom at all moments, teachers will have more spare time to perform certain assignments.

While the Classroom is available from a mobile computer, students, and teachers may use their phones and tablets to get active.

Communication

Teachers and students are allowed to send emails, post on the internet, provide private feedback on assignments, and receive job information. Teachers are totally in control of students' feedback and updates. They may also communicate with parents through individual emails or via

Classroom email summaries, which include dates and class announcements.

Collaborate

The curriculum provides several opportunities for students to interact together. Within the classroom, teachers will promote online discussions among students and construct group projects.

Moreover, students can work together to share Google Docs with teachers.

Engagement

Many digital natives are comfortable with technology and must be more likely to take responsibility and control of using technology. The classroom provides multiple means of rendering learning more engaging and constructive.

It enables teachers to differentiate assignments, integrate videos, and web sites into the classes and build collective community activities.

Differentiation

The teachers can clearly discern learners teaching through the Classroom. Assigning lessons to the entire college, specific students, or classes of students requires just a few required measures while creating a task on a Classwork website.

Feedback

An important aspect of all the training is to give the students positive input. Within the assessment resource at the Classroom, teachers will give each student input on assignments.

Within the rating process, there is also the ability to create a statement bank for future usage. The iOS device Classroom, in turn, lets users annotate work.

Data Analysis

To keep learning effective, instructors will evaluate data from the assessment and ensure the learners understand learning goals. Information from analyses may be forwarded easily to Sheets for storing and review.

CHAPTER 4:

Virtual Classes

Prepare Your Mind

A virtual educator is someone who has to teach day and night as different students live in different parts of the world. When you teach online, no matter what time of day you teach, don't show unnecessary details about your private life to your students.

The important thing here is that you teach with sincerity and show so much interest in the topics you teach. The quality of your teaching is reflected in your delivery.

Your student classroom can be spread from different parts of the world. Your student doesn't care if you had a good night's sleep or a bad day.

Engage your students with positivity from your attitude, voice, and mental attitude. Make sure your students get the best possible learning experience from you.

Being Flexible Is Key

Being flexible is crucial every time you are in front of your virtual audience. You may experience interruptions when information is not well received by your audience. Information cannot be received for various reasons, from technical to cultural. That is why flexibility is part of the solution. You must be able to adapt to the circumstances you experience.

Communicate Regularly and Provide Feedback

Your students can give you relevant feedback that can help move your entire class forward. Your students may have attended the online class more often than most. That experience can help educate you about the pros and cons of your overall online classroom.

In addition to your online students, you can also look for and connect with other online teachers. Keep in mind that education is a 'sharing' field. These connections can be invaluable for your online education development.

You see, online education is an excellent opportunity. The flexibility is an incredible benefit for teachers and students around the world. It is a growing market for virtual teachers and therefore an exciting career development opportunity.

How to Be a Virtual Communicator?

The art and science of communication is an essential part of being human. The exchange of information, thoughts, and ideas from person to person is communication. Humans have developed different communication processes to understand and express each other as the most intelligent animals on Earth. Not only do we have different ways of expressing oral communication; we also have nonverbal communication methods, such as facial expressions, gestures, and body movements.

We have used new technology to expand written and oral communication, which has led to the advent of a new form of communication, virtual communication, which simulates personal communication using technology.

Today, web-based services such as video conferencing and webcams make virtual communication commonplace. The people you talk to may be in the next room, another apartment nearby, or abroad. Today it is used in almost every way of life for family, friends, businesses, and online education.

In the past, writing decorum was considered suitable for electronic messages, now we have adopted a new way of communicating. Texting and messaging have evolved in a very interesting way over time with abbreviations like LOL and emojis making a big impact.

How Do Teachers Communicate Virtually?

Virtual education combines best practices from video production, video conference practices, and traditional teaching methods.

The teacher is often the subject of the video or stream while giving live online instruction. A subject is a person who holds the attention of the audience as an actor on stage. As a virtual teacher, you are not only an actor, but also the director who sets the scene, scripts the part and brings the setting, environment, and all components of a story to life.

Virtual communicators use a combination of oral, non-verbal, and written processes to transfer messages between parties via electronic media. Technology improves the way the subjects align mood, attitude, scene, and mood in ways that would otherwise be lost without being personal.

If you consider your class as a movie stage, you better prepare as a virtual teacher while delivering content in different virtual settings.

As a virtual educator, you need to look for ways in which technology can enhance or complement your students' experience. You can use live video and streaming technology to expand the billboards of your classroom to billions of students online.

Virtual teachers use the best of their environment, comparable to physical settings. Teachers in the classroom need to understand how to control the room. Getting and keeping your audience's attention is always a challenge for virtual teachers. Regardless of the circumstances, physical, or virtual; teachers are responsible for distributing instructions, guiding their research, and building their confidence.

Be a Better Virtual Communicator

Below are the main ways you can become a better virtual communicator:

Use different ways to express yourself

Virtual communication is not just about video and audio. As you can see on TV and film, each specific scene can dramatically change the mood, perception, and subsequent look at the actors' actions.

You are central to the classroom. Communicate a positive, upbeat attitude, and happy emotions to create a stimulating mental mood among your audience, in the classroom or on a webcam, TV, or stage.

Practicing the correct posture is key when standing in front of the camera. Make sure your back is straight and upright; your chin should be perpendicular to the floor and level with the camera.

Get instant feedback

The good thing about networking today is that it enables two-way communication. You can give and receive direct viewer feedback on the effectiveness and relevance of your material and delivery.

Feedback channels are great ways to capture your audience's thoughts and feelings. Feedback channels such as testimonials, reviews, and customer satisfaction departments are typically used by companies to correct courses and/or improve products. To improve your teaching quality and to support your students; you need to set up feedback channels at the beginning of your interaction.

Feedback channels in a virtual educational environment are likely to follow the example of any company or private institution. Customer reviews, thoughts, and constructive criticism should be welcomed by virtual teachers. You can concentrate the feedback by creating online surveys that are integrated into your courses.

In addition, feedback channels are created between customers and brands to provide real-time customer feedback. But always remember that feedback isn't always about direct comments, surveys, or specific to your development.

For example:

"I normally have a class with many active participants. However, when discussing the difference between past and present, no one took part in the online activity I had prepared. The change in behavior was a red flag. The content provided was ineffective or the way it was introduced.

Note which student actions in the previous example were considered the norm and how often that norm changed. Use the input to act accordingly in class and prepare for lessons. The teacher immediately identified a change in behavior regarding her instruction and a necessary change. We will bring up various feedback channels in this text.

One of the most typical feedback channels for virtual teachers today is electrical messages such as instant messaging (chat), texting, or emails. Anytime you can establish one-on-one communication with your students; it helps build trust and honesty.

Use exciting and eye-catching activities

You need to use unique and relevant technology resources to get your messages across, just like in any traditional classroom. Not all ideas will stimulate your audience, this is a trial and error method. Therefore, choose carefully and keep up with unique ways to keep students interested in the learning materials while online.

Attention and motivation can be easily influenced by audiences of all ages. The content you use will compete with current event alerts, specialized social media notifications, and a wave of free streaming entertainment. How will you compete? Why does your audience want to participate in the learning process that is currently taking place? How can the audience communicate with you to stay involved?

One way to get your students' attention and familiarize them with participation is to use virtual icebreakers. An icebreaker is an approach you can use to initiate conversations and remove embarrassment and barriers between your audience. Generally, icebreakers occur after introductions. You could use one before classwork puts everyone in a learning mood. Below are good examples of virtual icebreakers you can use:

- Find an activity that students can participate in by using items that members of the audience can find at home. This makes the activity cheap and fun for everyone.

- Interactive games and software where the public can participate in the promotion.

- Relevant songs and music (in whatever form).

- Ask the audience a question to respond via chat, comment, etc.

- Share your screen—some activities may not match the size of your class, but you can show your screen and participate in a game for them.

- All students choose topics for discussion. Find out what concerns them. (Note: This changes the spotlight and gives your audience the opportunity to be topics in class).

- Getting to know each other is a good icebreaker; introductions can be as long or short as you like.

Games are an excellent way to learn. Learning through fun and games has been receiving the undivided attention of the many target groups for a long time.

Integrate independent research as part of learning

Your audience should learn and understand how to use the tools they have on hand. A goal of modern researchers is to develop self-sufficient researchers.

You will find a wide variety of resources spread over the Internet. Your goal is to help your students decipher all this data. Knowing how to search the Internet for the best and worst sources of information is critical to gaining reliable and accurate knowledge of any topic. Incorrect information is prevalent on the internet. We help our virtual students to become independent researchers in their school work.

Maximize the time you have from start to finish

Don't waste screen time. As with any live production, the set is prepared before the cameras start rolling. Before you turn on the webcam, make sure you are as willing as possible to present your lesson, provide feedback, and answer questions.

Use the time you have with your students effectively. Our world is moving at a very fast pace. Respecting your audience's time is a golden rule for any teacher. In addition, punctuality and timeliness is a requirement for any virtual teacher who uses the Internet to complement the classroom environment.

Remember that good, engaging alternative learning materials will help fill in the time to the end of the lesson. It also helps to strengthen the material given during the lesson.

For example, keep flashcards, games, video, or some relevant learning material on hand for last-minute fill-ins. There will be times when you have planned a lesson and the planned material goes through faster than expected.

CHAPTER 5:

Getting Started with Google Classroom

While classrooms become more paperless, teachers need to find solutions for homework sharing, classroom management, student communication, and so on.

More and more teachers are coming to Google Classroom for smooth virtual classes that focus less on technology and more on teaching. You don't need to be a tech professional to lead this department.

Before you can make Google Classroom a part of your teaching experience, you need to make sure that you download the Google Apps for Education. This is a pretty simple process to go through and have work for you, but there are a few steps that you will need to work on first.

First, there are a few rules for who can get on the Google Classroom app. Any student, parent, or alumni group that has been registered as a 501(c) (3) can get on the Google Classroom app. Also, any accredited or non-profit K through 12 learning institutions can use this as well. You may want to consider talking to your administrator to see if this is a service that is already offered through your school or not.

Once you have checked in on this part, you will need to go through the following steps to sign up for the app:

- You will want to start by going to the sign-up form for the Apps for Education. You will be able to find it at https://www.google.com/a/signup/?enterprise_product=GOOGLE.EDU#

- Once you are on this page, you can fill the form in and then click on the Next button.

- From here, you will provide your institution's domain. If this isn't available, you can go through and purchase a new domain to help you get this started.

- Then click on Next and provide the rest of the information that is needed so that you can become an admin.

- Make sure to read through the Agreement before accepting and finishing the sign-up.

You may want to consider doing this a little bit early, like before school starts, because it can take up to two weeks before Google is done reviewing the application. After this time frame, you are going to receive your own acceptance form when the application is successful. You will now be able to verify your own domain as well as add addresses, mail integration, apps, and contacts to start using this. Keep in mind that you will not need to do this for each class, but you only need to go through this and do it one time. Once you are in, you will be able to assign different classrooms and have more than one in place under the same account.

From here, you will need to work on downloading the Google Classroom App. You will be able to go to the App Store and get this one just by looking for Google Classroom, or you can just visit Google Play and find it as well. Once you have downloaded this particular app; you will need to choose to sign in as the teacher. It is also possible to download an extension or a bookmark-like app that will work on Google Chrome. You just need to visit the Chrome Store to install all of this.

There are a few ways that you can install the Google Classroom App so that you can use it for your own needs. If you are considered the administrator; you will be able to install this extension by using the following steps:

- Visit the Google Admin Console.

- From here you will click on Chrome Management and then User Settings.

- Then you will be able to select the organizational unit that you would like to work with from here.

- Now you can click on Apps & Extension before clicking on Force Installed Apps & Extension. When you get to this point, click on Manage Force Installed App.

- Inside this tab, you will click on Chrome Web Store and then look for the series of letters that don't seem to make sense and click on those. If you can't find that, you can click on Share to Classroom.

- Now click the Add button that is right next to your extension before hitting save.

These steps are only if you are going to be the administrator. If you are using the Google Classroom through your educational institution, you will not need to go through the steps above because someone else will go through and do it. The steps that you will need to go through as a teacher, and that your students will need to go through as well, include:

Visit g.co/sharetoclassroom

When you get here, you can click on Add to Chrome and then click on the Add button.

From here, you can click on the icon that is next to the extension. You will need to make sure that you are signed in with Google before you do all of this.

And that is all that you will need to do to make sure that Google Classroom is downloaded for you and that you can use it for your classroom and your teaching experience. Since this is such a popular platform to work with, it is likely that your school already has this available for you to use for your classes, or they will be interested in learning more about it.

Now your class is ready! At least it is there, and anyone can access it. There are a few other things that need to be done before you go out.

Create your first project or create a message. You can share your first ad in Stream, or you can go to class. Click the "Create" button and share your first assignment in Google Classroom. Remember to count your projects. Make it easy for your students to see who comes first because you are unable to organize your tasks manually. However, you can move projects up. Click on the title to see if any students have completed the project and provide grades and feedback. Then you can give your students the tasks so they can start changing again.

Add teaching material to your project/class. Add content from Google Drive, or add a video from YouTube, files from your computer, links, and more. You can get these settings right on the right day. If you just want to share a presentation on your non-project-related class, go to the "about" file. Here you can add some teaching material such as slides, interesting articles, and examples.

Log in to the drive directory. Each time you create a new class, Google Classroom Drive creates a folder for that category. You can access the folder by going to all your class tiles. In each tile, you will find icons for the folder. Click on it, and you're in the folder. You can also add class material here. All of your students' tasks are automatically filled into the Google Drive folder, so you can get them back anytime you want.

CHAPTER 6:

Navigate Google Classroom

Navigation and Some Other Settings of Google Classroom

When you sign in to GC there is much to try for. You will have to know how to do navigate first. The very first page you will see, is the homepage of the Classroom, shows all of the classes that you have made or joined.

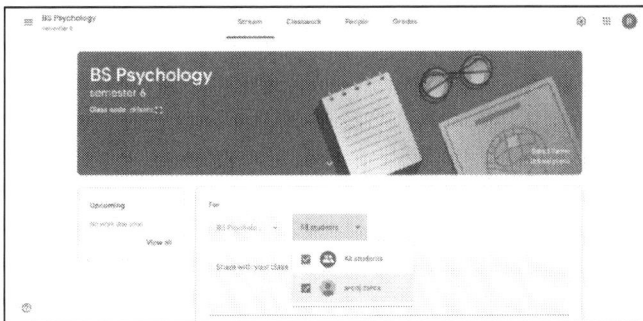

The Classroom Homepage

Class Tile: It displays the class name and student number on Google Drive, and also a link to the grade book and folder for the class files.

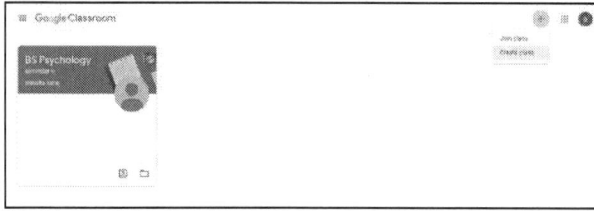

Creating or joining a class: Press the + to create a new class, or use a class code to join a class.

Google Apps: Jump into the suite for another Google app. The app you selected will open in a fresh browser tab.

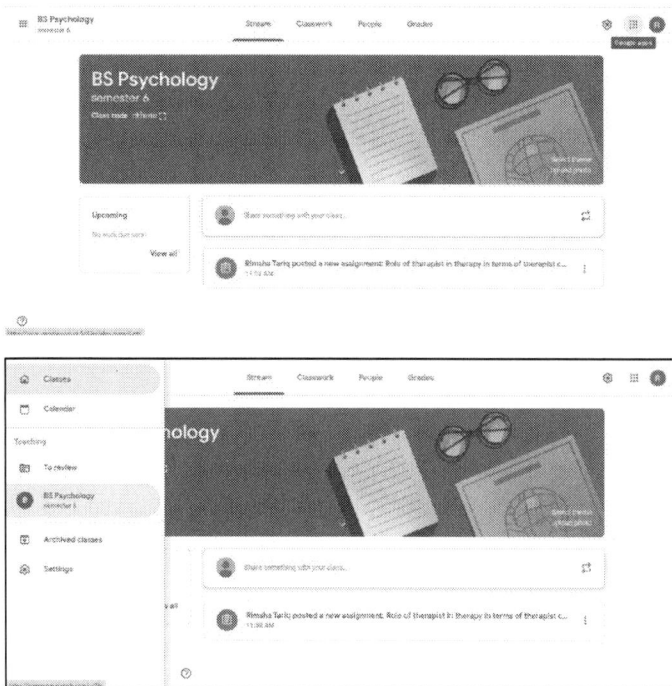

Menu: Provides options for adjusting viewpoints, switching to a class, or altering settings.

Google Account: Change settings of your Google Account by clicking on your image. You can open your Google Account tab, sign out, or attach another Google Account.

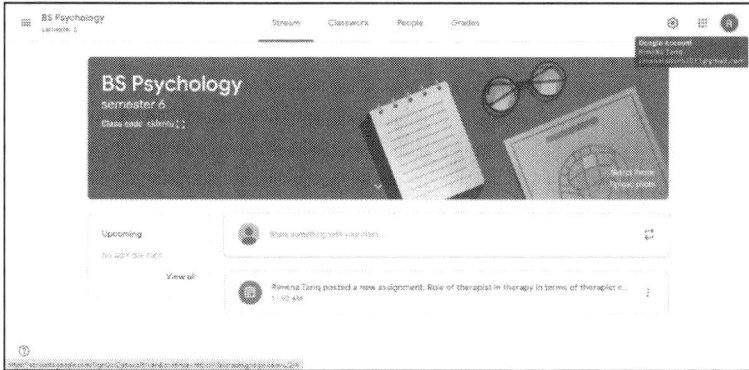

Sign: To see what's new, give your suggestions, inquire, or get support.

Google Classroom menu

Active Classes: The menu here shows the participating courses. Move to a class easily by clicking on them.

To-do: See the To-do page for an overview of questions and assignments across all of your classes. You will search by class and just display the job within a single class.

Calendar: Record class schedules for assignments, queries, and activities in the class calendar. You and the students will display a calendar image of the job for every semester.

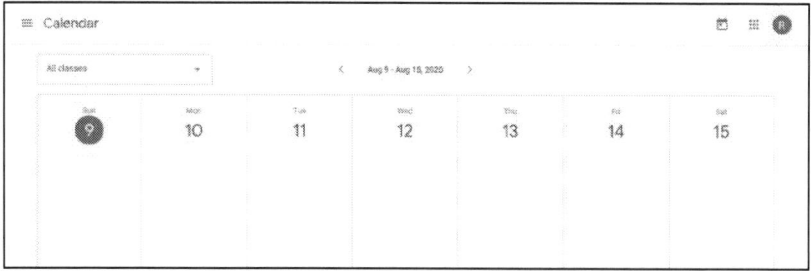

Classes: You have to see the GC homepage which displays the tile format of your classes that are active.

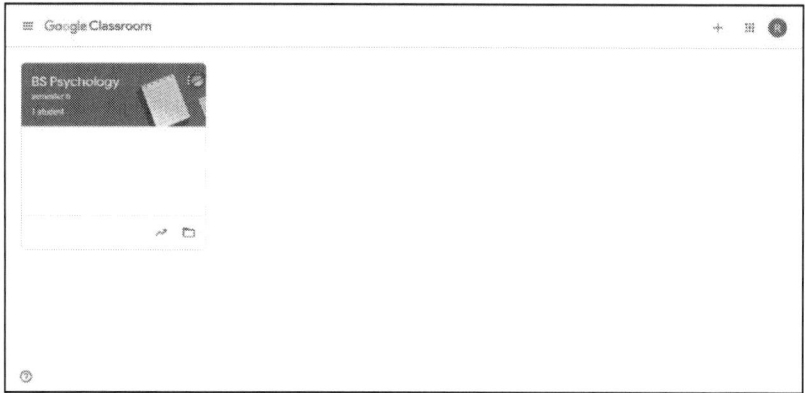

Archived Classes: Access the classes you were attending. Restore these groups or uninstall them right here.

Settings: Manage your account settings, change your profile, and adjust the email, comment, and classwork notifications. The settings available are Google Classroom wide settings affecting all classes that you are teaching.

How to Navigate Your Class?

To access a class click on the class page.

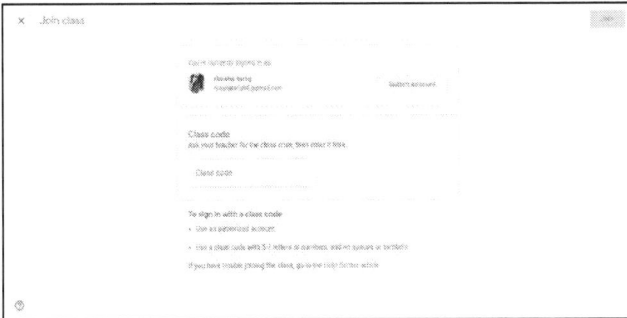

Upon joining a class, you can see the class code which students need to use, as well as four top tabs.

To jump to a class area, click a tab at the top of the page.

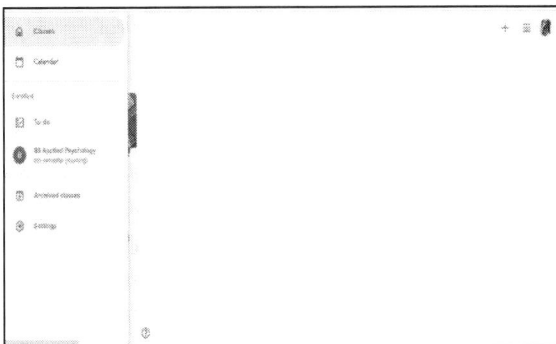

Classwork: That is where the submissions, queries, and class materials are made. In addition, to retain the Classwork page structured; you can create themes. You can create a topic, for example, one for homework, one for classwork, and another for the project. All like work will be structured under your assigned topic.

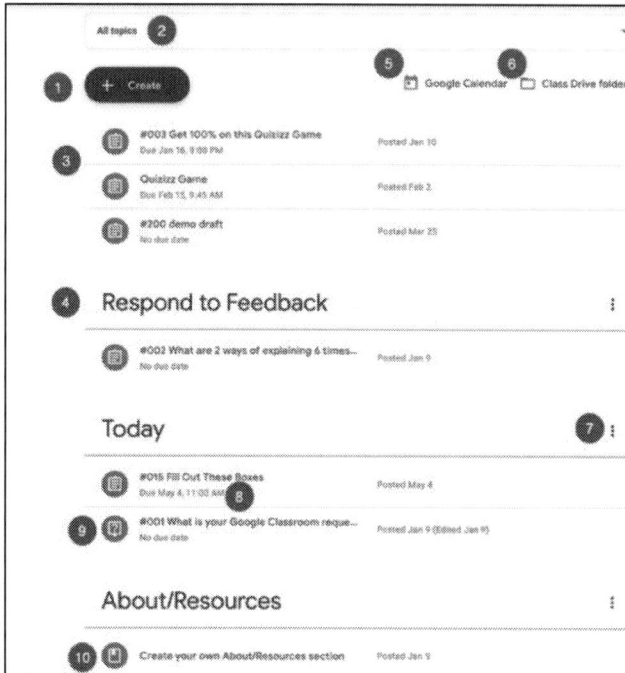

1. Create assignments.

2. Filter for topics.

3. Assignments without a topic.

4. Topic headings.

5. Class Google Calendar.

6. Class Google Drive folder.

7. Three Dots More menu for the topic.

8. Due Date and time.

9. Question assignment posted.

10. Materials posted.

Stream: This is a prime location for viewing announcements and class posts. That always occurs on the Stream as it is applied to the classwork. A list of submissions with the given upcoming dues dates is displayed on the left-hand side of the Stream page in the Next area.

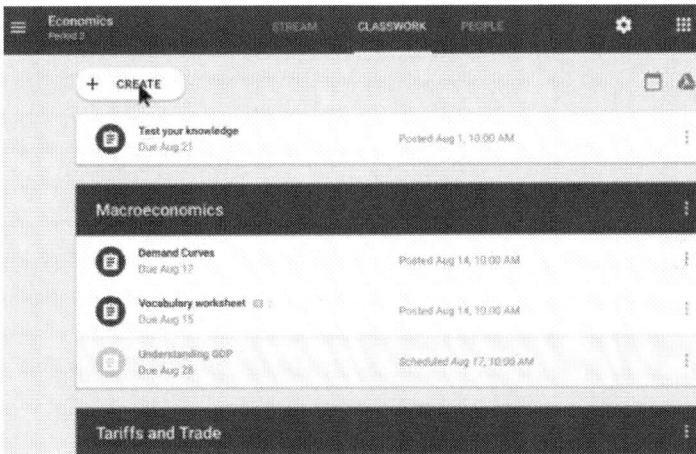

Grades: It includes viewing, grading, and returning assignments. You see both individual scores for students as well as the average class.

People: This tab holds a list of classes for both instructors and class co-workers. Further people can also be added to the class from here.

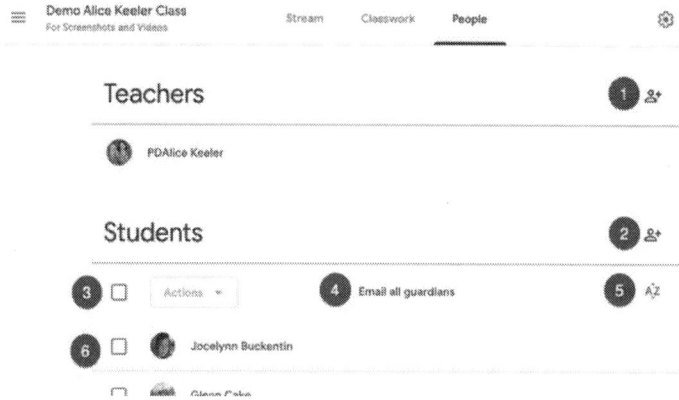

1. Add the co-teacher.

2. Via email invite a student.

3. Select all the students.

4. Email all the guardians.

5. Sort by the first name.

6. Select an individual student.

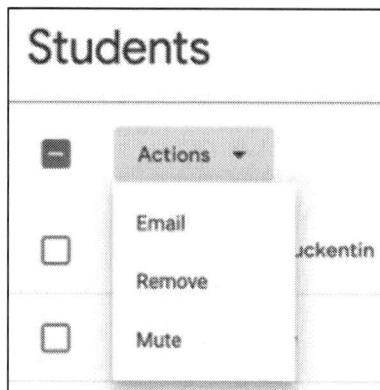

7. **Actions:** Email the selected student(s). Remove the selected students. Mute the selected students from posting to the class Stream.

You Can Handle or Change Class Details

Upon building a class, you can display or alter the specifics of your class. Facts of the curriculum include:

- General information, like class name, room number, and section

- The video meeting link in class

- Settings to your Stream tab for articles

- Your category code

The class settings can be updated on your Preferences tab. If you have various segments of the same class, modifications to a single class don't apply to others.

Edit a Class Section, Name, Room, Description, or Subject

A class name is needed. If you modify the class name, this will not automatically update the title of the class Drive folder. To update the name of the folder goes to your Drive class folder.

Go to the classroom.google.com.

Then click Settings and then click Class.

The class name is entered automatically.

Enter your changes under Class Details, and click Save.

Edit your class. In the student view, blank fields do not show.

Reset, Copy or Turn off The Class Code

When you build a class, Classroom generates a file for the lesson automatically. You can reset it if the students have difficulties with the class code. You can enable the code if you don't want to see new students joining your class. You can activate this at any time.

Once a class code is reset or activated, Classroom must generate some new code for your class. The preceding code works no longer.

Then, go to the classroom.google.com.

Next, click Settings and then click Class.

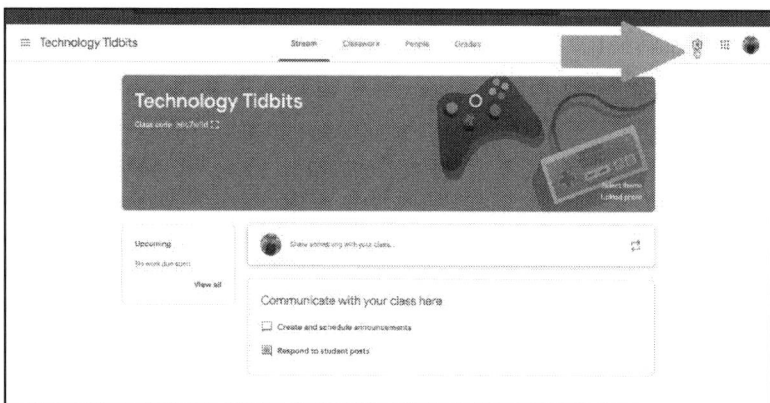

Under General, click the Down arrow next to the code of a class, and then choose an option:

Tap on Display to display the address.

Click Reset to reset the Code.

Click Disable or Activate to turn the code either off or on.

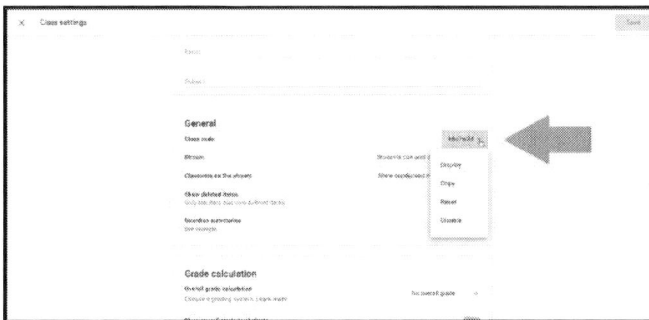

Click on Copy to copy code.

Then just click Save.

Choose How Classwork Notifications Show On the Stream Page

You may select how the Stream page shows alerts for your Classwork updates, and what information the alerts contain.

Go to the classroom.google.com.

Then click Settings and then click Class.

Click the Down arrow next to the Classwork on the page, and then pick an option:

Display details and attachments—students should see an updated update screen.

Show simplified alerts—Students display updates without information and attachments.

Hide Notifications—the Stream tab contains not any Classwork Notifications.

Click the Save button. Only teachers see totals turned in, graded, and assigned to an assignment.

To Note Deleted Student Posts

You will see any of the posts and comments a student-created and erased afterward.

Go to the classroom.google.com.

Then click Settings and then click Class.

Under General press the On or Off switch next to Show Deleted Objects.

Click the Save button.

CHAPTER 7:

How to Set-up Google Classroom

Creating and Setting Classes

Getting into Google Classroom is really easy. You just have to access by logging in to classroom.google.com you can use your personal email or email specifically for your profession.

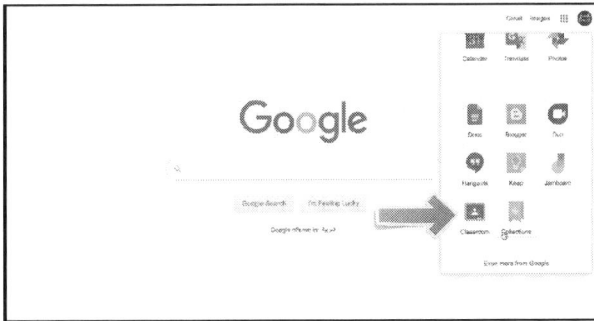

By the upper right portion, there is an icon of "+," and by pressing that; we can create a class if we are a teacher or join a class if we are a student.

To create a class, we can choose a class, sector, subject, and classroom name. Because of this, students would be able to identify their classes and subjects easily. From there, the class would then be created and the

Class Code would be available that can be used to invite students.

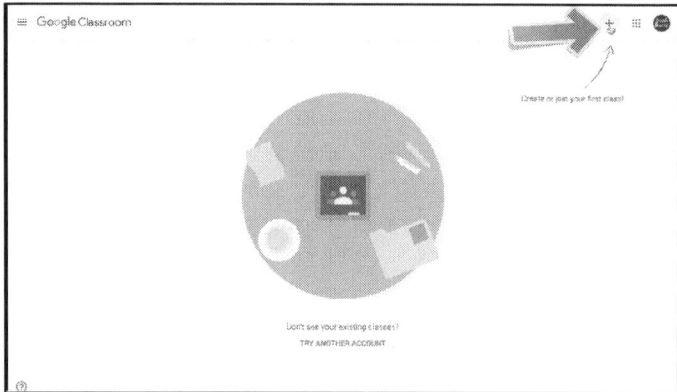

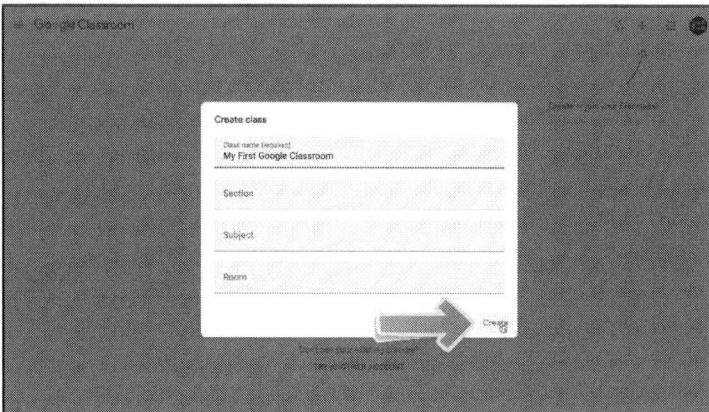

Inviting Your Students on Google Classroom

There are two ways you can invite students into your Google Classroom: by displaying class code or by inviting them directly.

Well, to invite students by class code, log into your Google Classroom. Select a classroom where you would like to invite your students to. Your class code is displayed right underneath your name, click on Display, and make sure that the class code is visible to your students. You can either project it onto the screen or simply write it on the board.

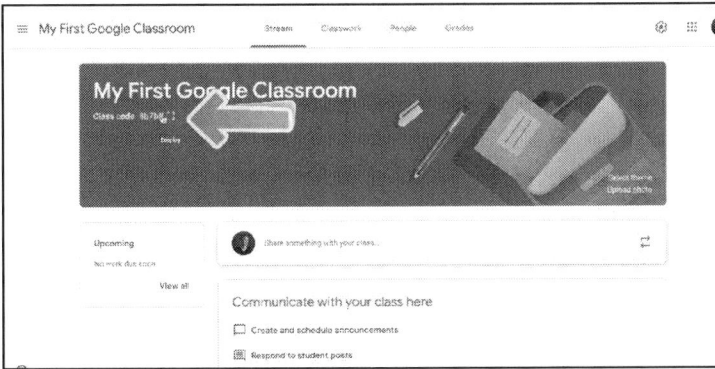

Instruct your students to sign into Google using their school Gmail accounts. Instruct your students to go to Google classroom, click the plus button in the top right corner. This is the time where they will insert a class code. Once they finished, click join. That's it; a student has successfully joined your Google Classroom.

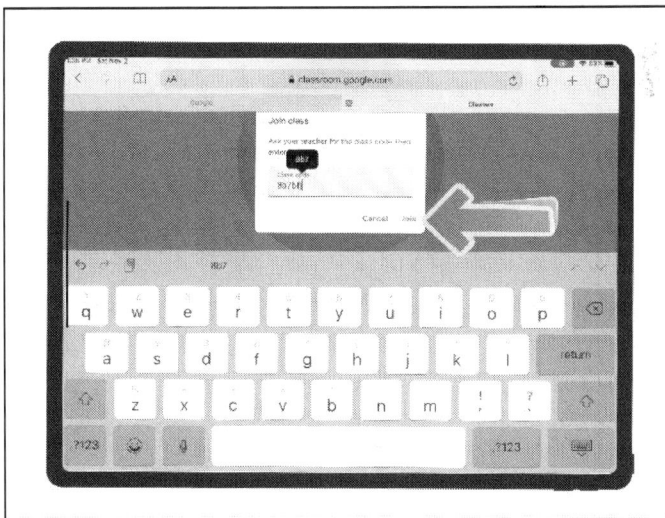

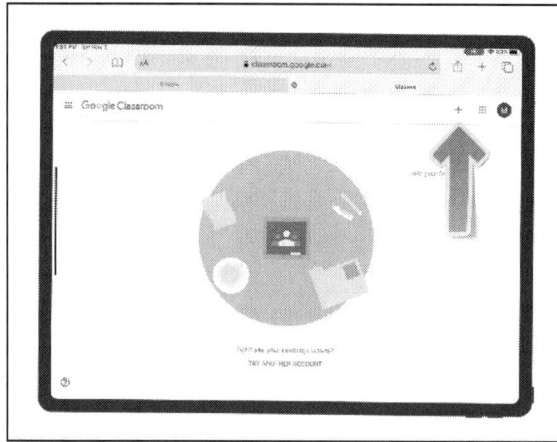

A direct invitation is another way to populate your Google Classroom. To do that, open your Google classroom, select a class where you would like to invite your students to go to the "people" tab. Find sign invite students and click on it. This is the field where you will paste or type names or emails of the students who you would like to invite. Once you've finished, click invite. Once the invitation has been sent; you will see the name of the students grayed out. They have received the invitation but have not joined a class yet.

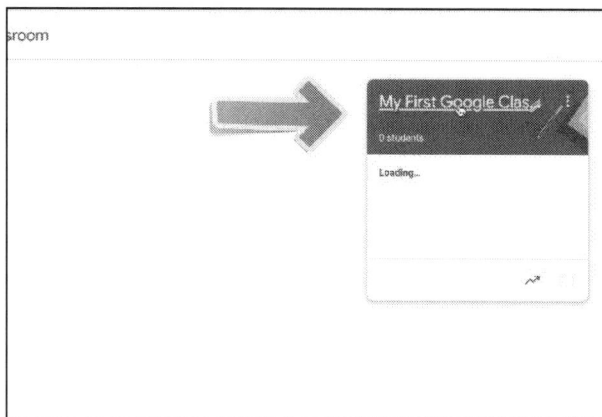

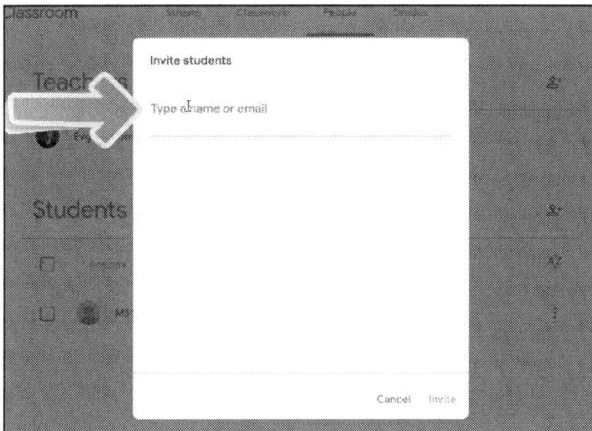

Instruct your students to login into Google using their school accounts. Once they've logged in, instruct them to go to Google Classroom. Once there, they should be able to see a Google Classroom, which you have invited them to. In my case, it's my first Google Classroom. The final step they need to take is to click join. That's it. Your student has successfully joined your Google Classroom by direct invitation.

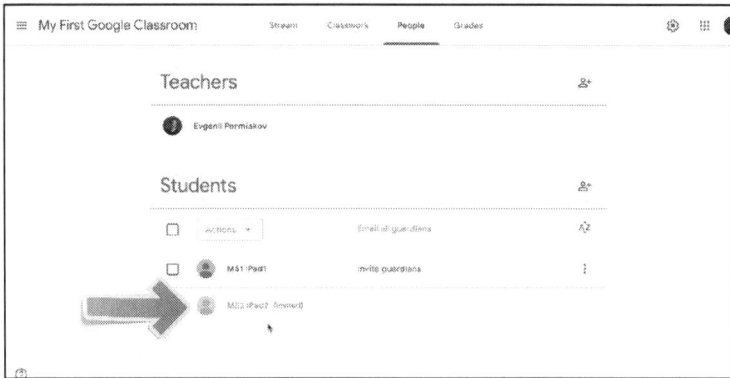

In the teachers' view to see what has changed and name that used to be grayed out is now solid black. If the name still appears light gray, it means that a student has not yet accepted your invitation.

How to Create and Collect Assignments/Tasks from Students

To create an assignment, go to classwork and click 'Create assignment'. Give your assignment a title, type up instructions for your students. Select whether your assignment will be ungraded or graded. Select a due date for your assignment.

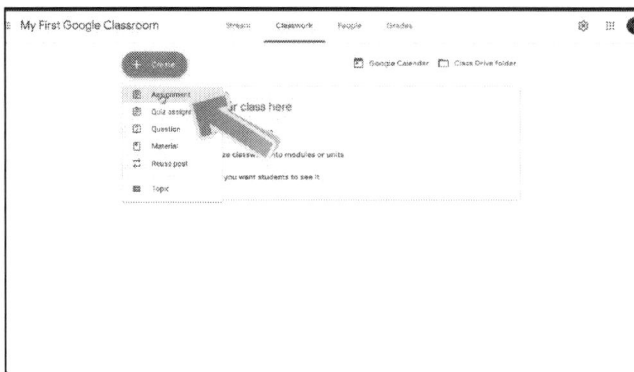

There are four kinds of supplementary materials that you can attach to your assignment.

The first one is an attachment from your computer or a file; the second one is a file from your Google Drive.

The third one is a YouTube video clip. The fourth is linked to any resource found on the internet.

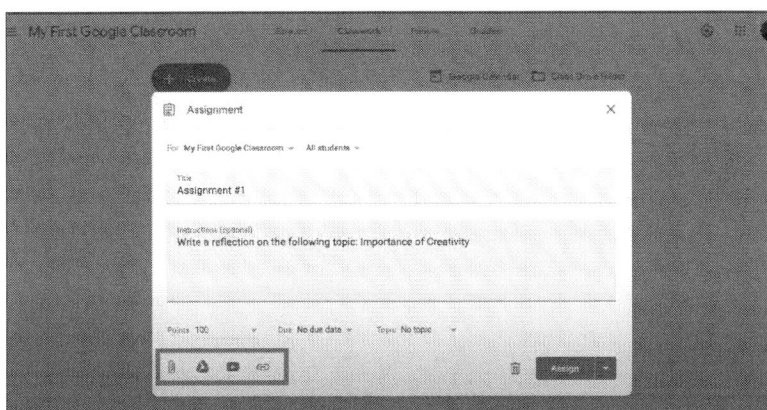

Finally, I would like my students to be able to reflect on all the materials they've watched. For this purpose, I created a Google Doc. So I will click on the second icon and select a Google Doc that I've recently created for this assignment. Select the file from your Google Drive and click add.

One important thing you need to remember when assigning Google Docs to your classes is to select the appropriate sharing type wherein the students can view the file; students can edit the file, and make a copy for each student.

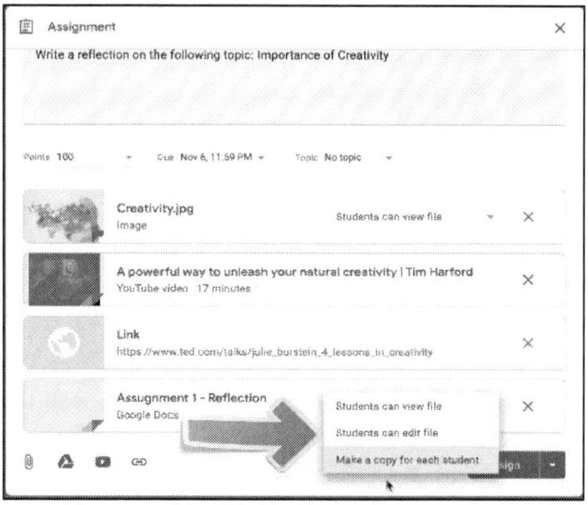

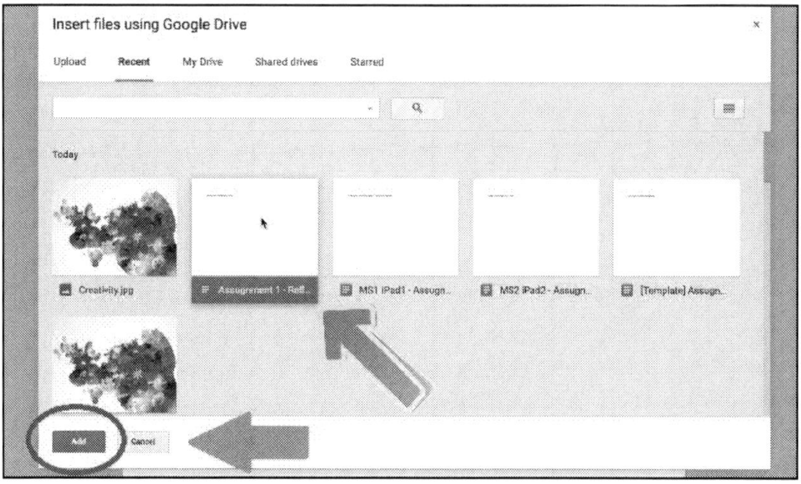

How to Use Question

The first thing you need to do is to go to classwork from your Google Classroom home screen. From there, select Create, select question. This is how we start a discussion board.

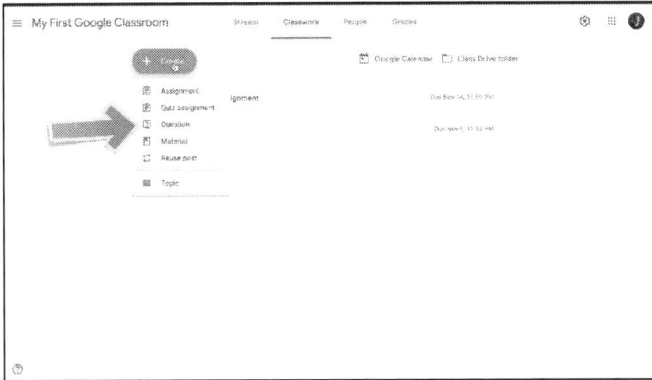

The first thing we need to think about is what it is that we want our students to talk about. And this is going to be our question. Well, in my case, I want my students to do discuss a video clip I found on YouTube about 'creativity'. So, this is going to be my question 'share your insights about the attached video', I'm going to click on YouTube sign and attach the video clip that I would like my students to discuss, share, insights, select the clip, click Add. So, I have my question. I have my clip here. And the other thing we need to select is how the students will answer this question. We have two options. We can either accept short answers or multiple choices. Well, in our case, we want to start a discussion board. So short answer makes more sense.

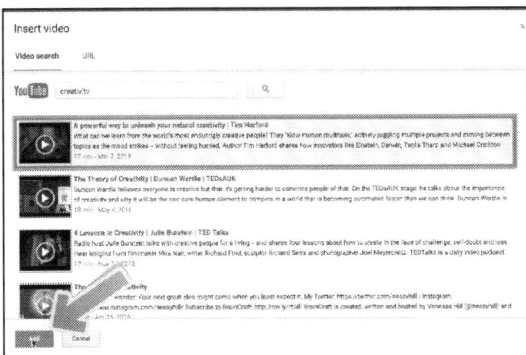

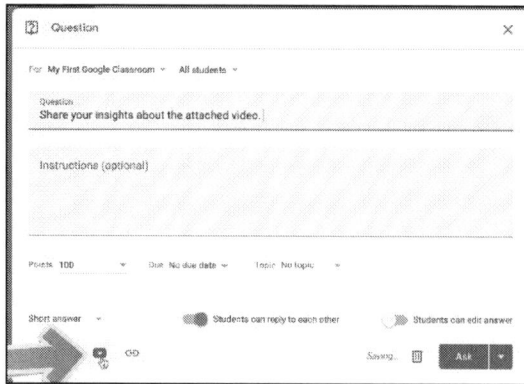

Make sure you enable students to reply to each other and students can edit the answer. This option lets students go back and edit the answers after they've been posted in case they've made a mistake, they can go back and edit. Select classes that you want to assign this question to. We can either ask now, in this case, the assignment will post it right away. We can schedule this assignment for later use, or we can save as draft and maybe ask it later or edit it later. In my case, I'm going to ask it now.

After you've asked your question; it's going to appear onto your classwork or in your stream.

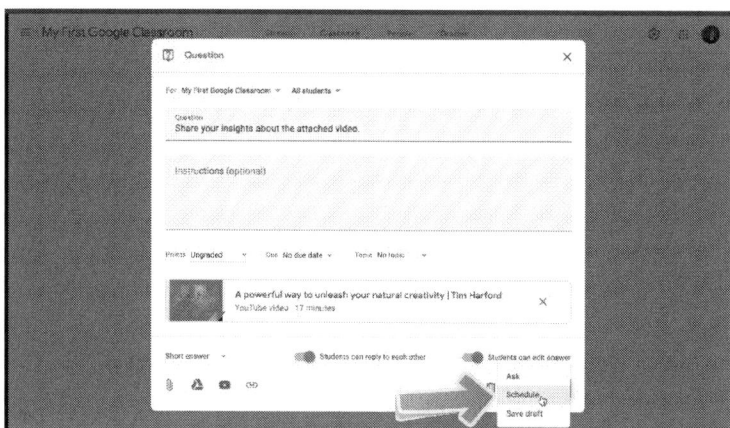

The question can be found right at the top, and I can do three things. I can add a class comment, I can type my answer, or I can add a private comment. And these three things are slightly different from each other. The question was to share my insights about the video attached. So, my insight would be this video is great. I'm going to click turn in. And you will notice that once I've turned in, I can now see classmate's answers if I click on it. I can also see how many replies I have right here.

How to Use Evaluation Tool/Rubrics

If we go to the assignment, you will see a new sign has been added to the user interface to the right of the topic. The first thing you need to do is create a title because I don't have any rubrics, I'm going to create a rubric from scratch.

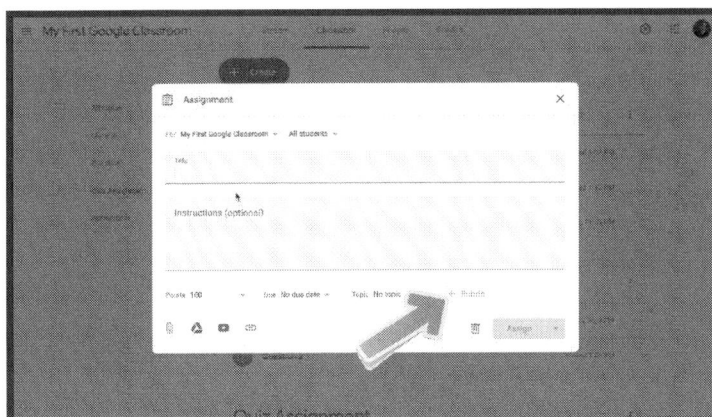

I'm going to be using this rubric for grading student tests. So, my first criteria are going to be word choice. I'm going to assign three points for level three. And this is going to be a description, accurate use of vocabulary. My second level is going to cost three points, it is going to be level two, and the description will be the average use of vocabulary. My third level is going to give the student one point; it's going to be level one, and the description will be a poor use of vocabulary. To add a level, we click on the plus button to the leader level; we need to click on three dots and delete level.

So, my first criteria is ready, I can add a new criteria and if I click that, a new field will be generated for another criteria or what I can do I can duplicate this criteria and just change word choice. I will change it to grammar and tweak my description a little bit at first description will be accurate use of vocabulary.

The second description is going to be average; I can duplicate the grammar and choose 'Opinion'. The first level is going to work for point, then three, two, and one. Google rubrics automatically generate the top score. I have three points in word choice, three points in grammar, and four points and opinion, which gives me 10 points. Once my rubric is ready, I'm going to click Save.

Once you save the rubric; it will be viewable in the assignment, you can click on the rubric, and then it will appear. You have an option to clear the criteria, expand them one by one, or expand them all at once. Once your assignment is ready, click 'assign'. The assignment has been generated.

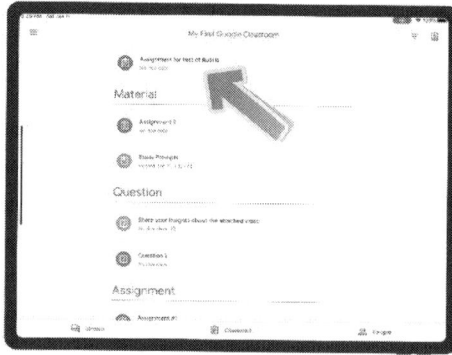

So from the teacher screen, click on 'turned in' and see the student's submission. My rubric will appear on the right-hand side of my screen. I can expand each level and market accordingly. So, what we've done right now, we've looked at student work, and we've marked it at the same time using our rubric, you will notice that Google rubric has generated the total score of seven out of 10. Based on the levels that we have selected. What it didn't do, however, it didn't transfer the rubric score into the grade. Google's rubric automatically transfers the rubric score to the final grade.

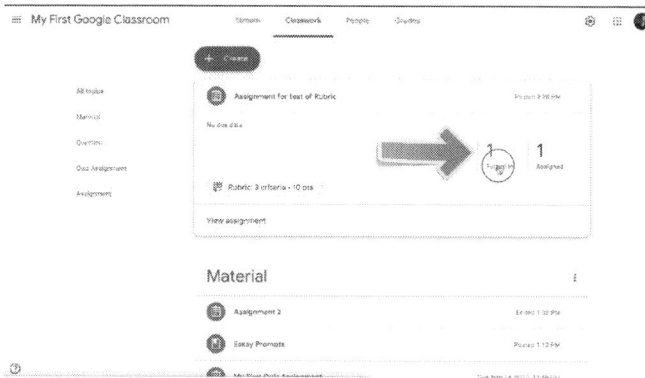

Use Stream

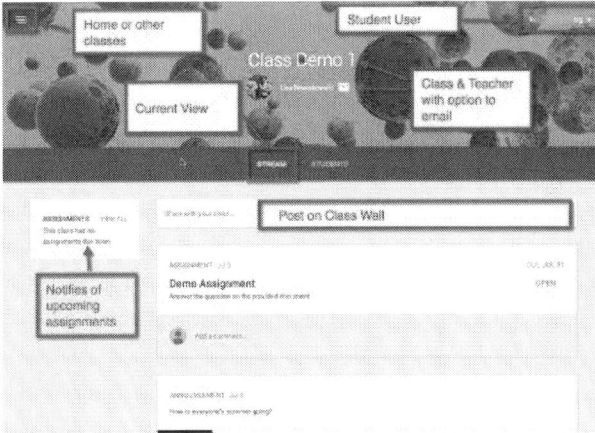

Here are some things you can do in streaming:

- **Post**—you can post your thoughts about certain information and even post your question in the stream of your class.

Examples:

What was our last discussion all about?

- **Comment**—you could respond to people who posted and comment about it.

We talked about addition in Mathematics.

- **Reply**—this is a response directly to the person who commented, especially in your own post

Example: commenter's name. Thanks!

Copy a Course

One of the nice things that a teacher will be able to do with Google Classroom is that they can take some of the posts that they used before, in another class or in a preceding class, and then reuse them a bit. This can be announcements, assignments, and even questions from their preceding classes to help them keep up with the work, especially if the information still works with this current class.

For the students, it is possible to go through and see some of the old classes that they were in. This can be helpful if you need to evaluate something that is inside of the older class or you want to get ahold of some papers or discussions that you want to use from a past semester. You just need to go through some of your past archived classes to find what you would like.

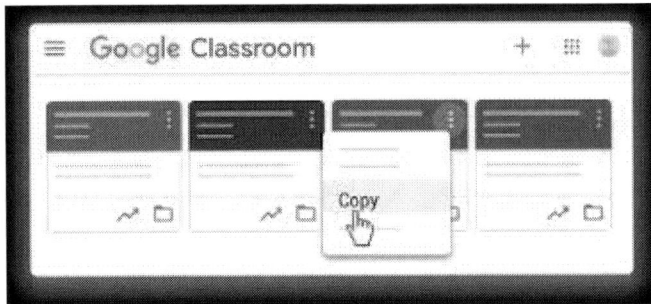

CHAPTER 8:

How to Set Due Date, Manage Homework, and Assignments?

Assignments are a useful tool on Google Classroom for delivering, tracking, and also grading student submissions. Even submissions that are non-electronic can also be tracked using the Assignments tool.

Add an Assignment

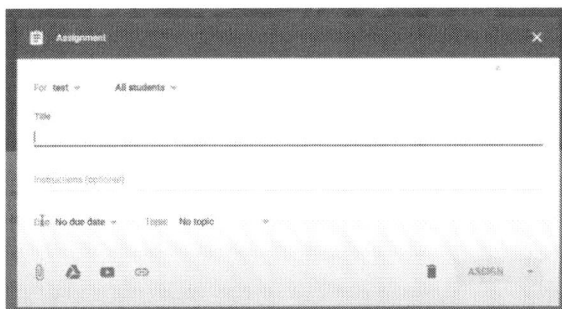

Creating an Assignment

- Open www.classroom.google.com.

- At the top, click on "Class" and open "Classwork."

- Also, click on "Create" and click on "Assignment."

- Input the title and necessary instructions.

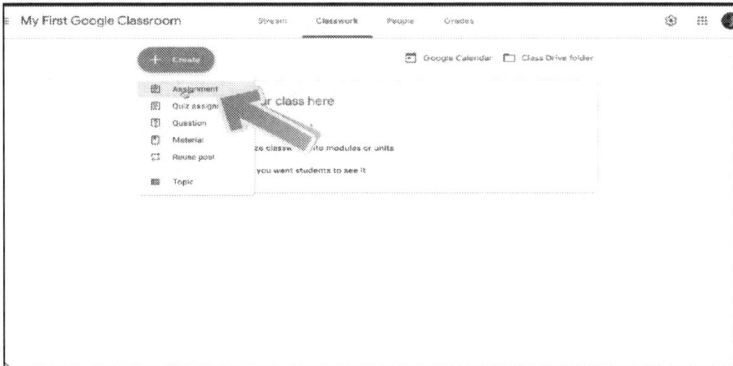

Inputting grade category

- Click the drawdown on "Grade Category."

- Select "Category."

- Edit the following (Optional).

- Click "Grades" to edit the grades page.

- Click "Instructions" to compose the Assignment.

- Click "Classwork" to create a homework, quiz, and test.

Change the point value

- Click the drawdown below points.

- Create a new point value or click "ungraded."

Edit due date or Time

- Click on the drawdown below "Due."

- Click on the dropdown on "No due date."

- Fix date on the Calendar.

- Create due Time by clicking Time, input a time adding AM, or PM.

Add a topic

- Click on the drawdown below Topic.

- Click on "Create Topic" and input the topic name.

- Click on an existing topic to select it.

Insert Attachments

File

- Click on "Attach."

- Search for the file and select it.

- Click "Upload."

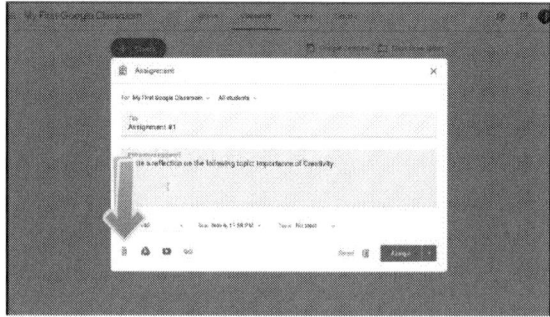

Drive

- Click on "Drive."

- Search for the item and click it.

- Click "Add."

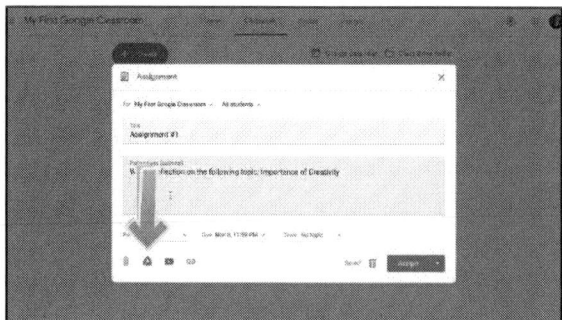

YouTube

- Click on YouTube.

- Type in the keyword on the search bar and click search.

- Select the video.

- Click "Add."

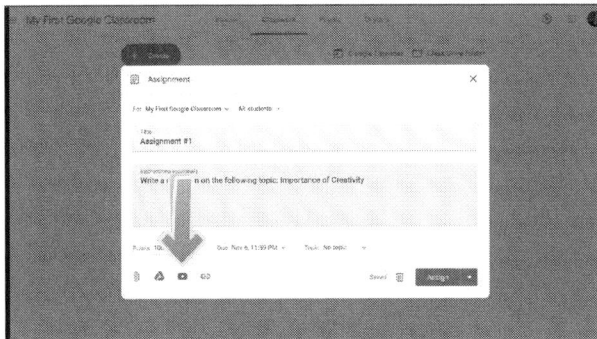

Link

- Click on Link.

- Select the URL.

- Click on "Add link."

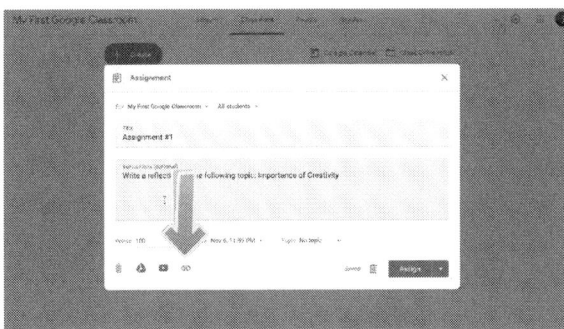

You can delete an attachment

- Click removes or the cross sign beside it.

You can also determine the number of students that interacts with the Attachment:

- Click on the drawdown besides the "Attachment."

- Select the required option.

- Students can View File—this implies that students are allowed to read the data but cannot edit it.

- Students can edit the file—this means students can write and share the same data.

- Make a personal copy of each student—this means students can have their transcript with their name on the file and can still have access to it even when turned in until the teacher return it to them.

Note: If you encounter an issue like, no permission to attach a file, click on copy. This will make the Classroom make a copy, which is attached to the Assignment and saved to the class Drive folder.

Add a Rubric

You must have titled the Assignment before you create a rubric.

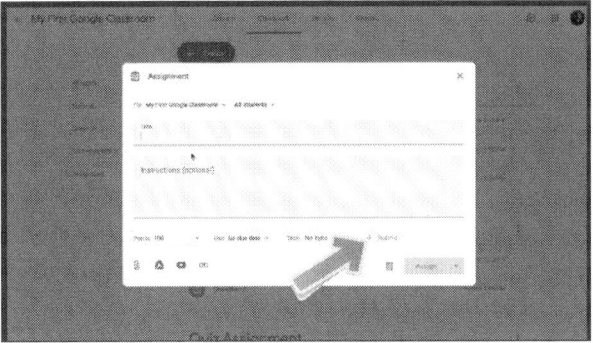

- Click the "Add" sign beside Rubric.

- Click on "Create rubric."

- Turn off scoring by clicking the switch to off, besides the Use scoring.

- Using scoring is optional, click "Ascending or Descending" beside the Sort the order of points.

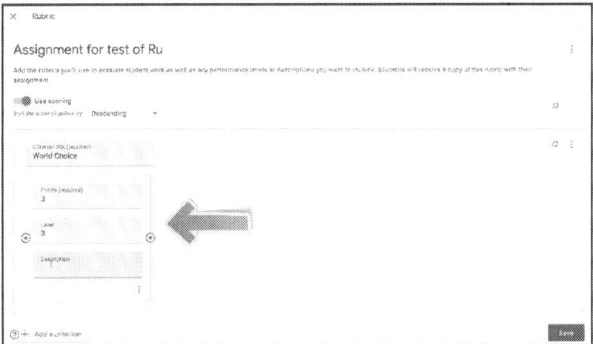

Note: using scoring, gives you the room to add a performance level in any with the levels arranged by point value automatically.

- You can input Criterion like Teamwork, Grammar, or Citations. Click the criterion title.

- Add Criterion description (Optional). Click the Criterion description and input the description.

Note: You can add multiple performance level and Criterion.

- Input points by entering the number of points allotted.

Note: The total rubric score auto-updates as points are added.

- Add A level title, input titles to distinguish performance level, e.g., Full Mastery, Excellent, Level A.

- Add a Description, input expectations for each performance level.

- Rearrange Criterion by clicking "More" and select "Up or Down."

- Click "Save" on the right corner to save Rubric.

Reuse Rubric

- Click on the "Add" sign beside "Rubric."

- Click "Reuse Rubric."

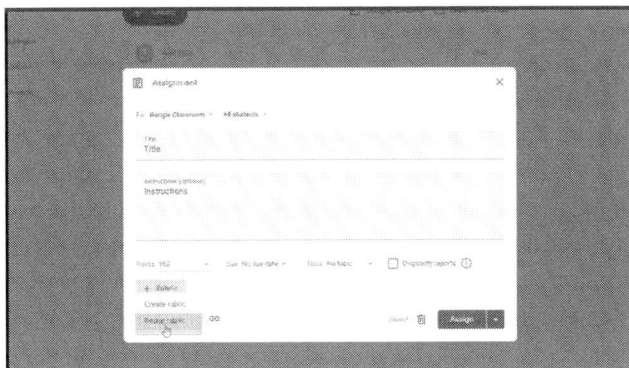

- Enter "Select Rubric" and click on the title. You can select Rubric from a different class by entering the class name OR by clicking the drawdown and select the Class.

- View or Edit rubric, click on "preview," click on "Select and Edit" to edit, save changes when it's done. Go back and click "Select to view."

View Rubric Assignments

- Click on "Rubric."

- Click the arrow up down icon for Expand criteria.

- Click the arrow down up icon for Collapse criteria.

The grading rubric can be done from the Student work page or the grading tool.

Sharing a Rubric

This is possible through export. The teacher creates the Rubric exports, and these are saved to a class Drive called Rubric Exports. This folder can be shared with other teachers and imported into their Assignment.

The imported Rubric can be edited by the teacher in their Assignment, and this editing should not be carried out in the Rubric Exports folder.

Export

- Click on "Rubric."

- Click "More" on the top-right corner and enter "Export to Sheets."

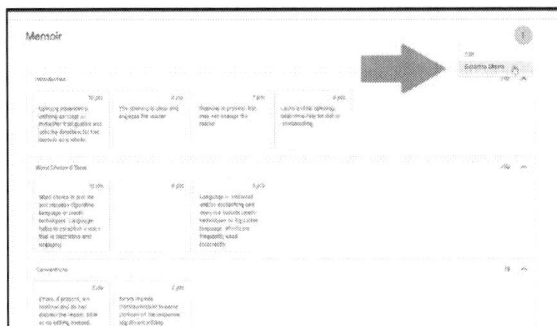

- Return to Classwork page by clicking close (cross sign) at the top-left corner.

- At the top of the Classwork page, click on Drive folder and enter My Drive.

- Select an option, to share one rubric, right-click the "Rubric." To share a rubric folder, right-click on the folder.

- After right-clicking, click on Share and input the e-mail you are sharing to.

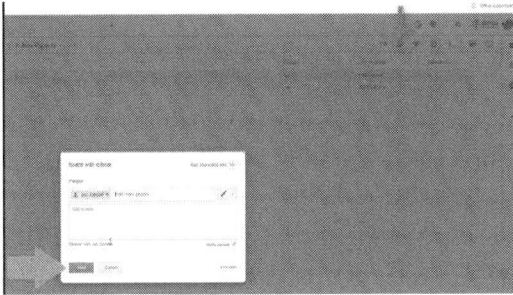

- Then click "Send."

Editing Rubric Assignment

- Click on the "Rubric."

- Click on "More" at the top-right corner and enter "Edit."

- Click "Save" after making changes.

Deleting Rubric Assignment

- Click on "Rubric."

- Click on "More" at the top-right corner and enter "Delete."

- Click "Delete" to confirm.

Posting, Scheduling, or Saving Draft Assignment

Post

- Open Classwork and click on Assignment.

- Click on the drawdown beside Assign, on the top-right corner.

- Click on Assign to post the "Assignment."

Schedule

- Click on the drawdown beside "Assign," on the top-right corner

- Enter "Schedule."

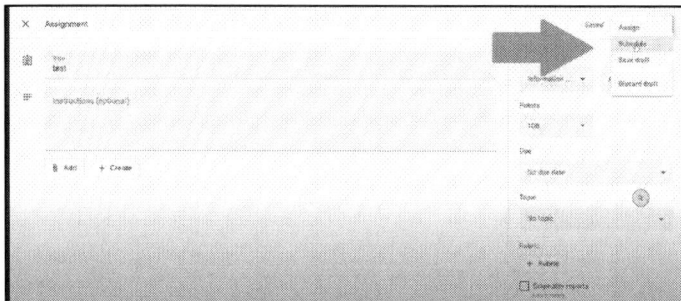

- Input and the date you want the "Assignment" posted.

- Click "Schedule."

Save

- Click on the drawdown beside Assign, on the top-right corner.

- Enter "Save Draft."

- Editing "Assignment:"

- Open "Classwork."

- Click on "More" (three-dot) close to "Assignment:" and enter "Edit."

- Input the changes and save for posted or schedule "Assignment," while Go to Save draft, to save the draft assignment.

Adding Comments to Assignment

- Open "Classwork."

- Click "Assignment" and Enter "View Assignment."

- Click on "Instructions at the top."

- Click on "Add Class Comment."

- Input your comment and Post.

To Reuse Announcement and Assignment

Announcement

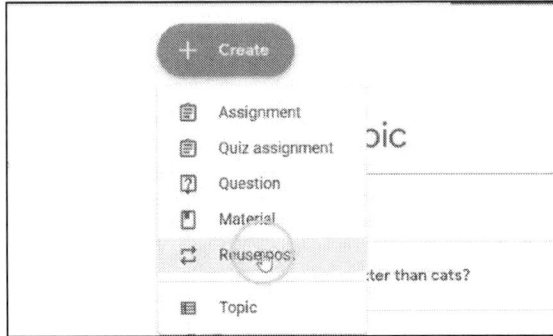

- Open the Class.

- Select "Stream."

- Slide into the Share something with your class box and click on a square clockwise up and down arrow or "Reuse" post.

Assignment

- Open "Classwork" and click on "Create."

- Click on a square clockwise up and down arrow or "Reuse" post.

- Select the "Class and Post" you want to reuse.

- Then click on "Reuse."

Delete an Assignment

- Open "Classwork."

- Click on More (three-dot) close to "Assignment."

- Click on "Delete" and confirm it.

Creating a Quiz Assignment

- Open "Classwork" and click on "Create."

- Click "Quiz Assignment."

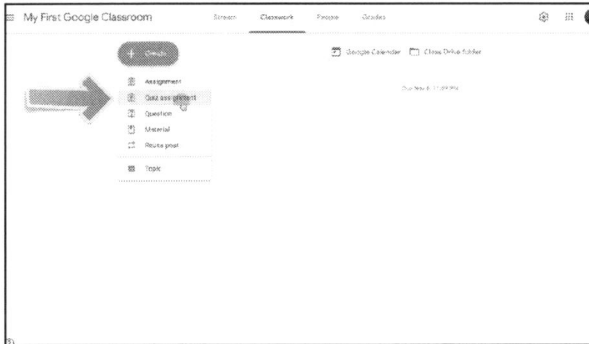

- Input the title and instructions.

- You can switch on Locked mode on Chromebooks to ensure the student can't view other pages when taking the quiz.

- You can switch on "Grade Importing" to import grades.

Response and Return of Grades

Response

- Open "Classwork."

- Click on "Quiz Assignment" and free "Quiz Attachment."

- Click on "Edit" and input "Response."

Return

- Open "Classwork."

- Click on "Quiz Assignment."

- Pick the student and click on "Return."

- Confirm "Return."

CHAPTER 9:

Difference between Google Classroom and other Platforms

L et's talk about Google Classroom versus Apple Classroom. Google Classroom is the focus of this book, but how does it stack up to Apple Classroom? Well, read on to find out.

The Hardware Differences

The biggest difference that you'll run into is the hardware elements. Apple Classroom is free for iPad, and the classroom involves using multiple different iPads, and the teachers will put these on the device, allowing students to use them as an integrative tool. The teacher iPad is a collection of these powers, in order to give a learning experience. Essentially, it's similar to Google Classroom, and once it is configured; it's connected to devices and the iPad is shared. Then once the session is done, it can be signed out of. It's a way to keep students focused, shows students different screens, and it can share documents with the class through the use of AirDrop. It shows student work on Apple TV, resets the passwords for students, creates groups of students based on the apps they use, and allows teachers to create groups and teams.

Basically, it's a way to have Apple within the classroom, and through the use of the iPad; it's more collaborative directly within the direct learning atmosphere.

Good for Lower Level Grades

Now you'll notice immediately that the only similarity is that they both include the word "classroom." This means that Apple Classroom is more of a direct classroom tool, and it helps teachers show apps and pages to students who might have trouble with them, and shows off the work that's there. Teachers in upper grades benefit from this because it monitors the activity, but the thing is, students can find out if the teacher is watching very quickly. It's more of a direct device to use for learning within the classroom, whereas with Google Classroom, focuses on both in and outside the classroom.

Google Classroom Focuses on Organization

One big part of Google Classroom is the organization element. It is all collaborated with Google drive, which means that learning is based on connections and education is based on the organization rather than directly in a physical classroom. Google Classroom makes it easy for teachers to assign the work and allows students to have better organization for assignments. It also allows them to get updates faster. You get the opportunity to go paperless too, which is a big plus. Google Classroom focuses on showing work that needs to be done, any grades they have, and any assignments that they missed. It's more of a tool for better organization of the student body over everything else.

Apple Classroom Has More Interactive Lessons

For those teachers who want to have a more engaging class, that's where Apple Classroom may work better. For example, if you're teaching a younger crowd, it may be better to have Apple Classroom because let's face it, do first graders really need to navigate Google drive and submit documents? Course not. They would benefit more from Apple Classroom, since it involves showing the app, and allows teachers to teach and students to focus on what the teacher is teaching. It's focused as well on interacting with the student, and it shows the assignment that they work on; giving teachers a chance to look at each of the pieces of work that the student does, and the most recently used options. There even the screen view that shows the iPad, and it is a good way to keep the direct focus of the students within the classroom.

So, if you're a more interactive-lesson focused teacher, such as you're teaching students the colors, or want students to not screw around in class; the Apple Classroom device may be a better option for you. If you're a teacher who is more interested in having essays, homework, and other elements easily organized in one place, then yes, Google Classroom may be more your style.

Google Classroom Allows For Multiple Devices to Be Used

It is possible to get tablets for Google Classroom, but if you want to have students work on something right away; they totally can. The beauty of Google Classroom is that it's not attached to a brand. You can get Google on your computers and installing chrome is super easy. With that, you are given way more options on using it. Google Classroom can be downloaded as an app too on your device, meaning that if you've got a phone, tablet, or whatever; you're essentially free to use it with whatever you want. That's what's so nice about it, because students can work on assignments right away, and from there, submit it to the teacher. It is also possible for students to work on different subjects while on the go and they can share different questions and resources with the teacher. This is much more interactive, and is perfect for a classroom with multiple smart devices.

The problem with Apple is that it's a brand. You are essentially working only with the Apple brand, meaning that it's highly limited. After all, not everyone may have a Mac or an iPad, so it doesn't really have as much use as say, Google Classroom does.

You Don't Have To Choose

The reality of this though, is that there are some key differences, and you can choose based on needs, with Apple classroom being more of a focus directly within the class environment itself, and Google classroom being more on workflow and assignments. They're two different tools, but comparing it is like comparing apples with oranges, which is a bit different from your average device comparison, since they are often pitted against each other in the technology realm. The truth is you shouldn't have to choose between them, because some teachers benefit from both. If you really want to make your classroom the best it can be, sometimes the best answer is to add both of these services, since they're both really good at what they do, and they complement each other well. The answer is you shouldn't choose one or the other. If you want to get both, get both. If the district can handle both, get both. But, if you're a teacher for a younger group of students, Apple Classroom works. If you're a teacher for older students, Google Classroom works.

Apple Classroom and Google Classroom are two very different types of software, but both of them accomplish the goal of helping children learn better, so they can use these skills to better their lives now and in their futures learning endeavors and studies that they will embark on.

CHAPTER 10:

Best Extensions for Both Teachers & Students

The greater part of the advanced student work is done inside an internet browser. On the off chance that you are in school or college, odds are a large portion of your work, and examining is additionally done in the program.

In this segment, I will manage you through the absolute best Chrome extensions each student must-have. A portion of these will assist you with getting progressively gainful; some will assist you with forestalling botches in your composition.

These Google Chrome extensions are allowed to introduce and the applications are excessively simple to utilize.

Grammar & Spelling Tools

Grammarly

Grammarly is a propelled language checking tool that tests your composition against several linguistic mix-ups.

The free form of this application will assist you with forestalling linguistic slip-ups in the vast majority of your composition. Another exceptional thing about this extension is that it chips away at a large number of the sites which incorporate Google Gmail Record, Google Doc, and some more. It can't be contrast with most other sentence structure tools, since it gives the choice for you to choose which English you compose—regardless of whether American or English.

The exceptional variant of this application won't just assist you with checking for language structure botches, however, it will likewise assist you with checking your content against counterfeiting. It additionally causes you to set a pace for your composition and proposes alterations as needs to be.

Language Tool

Language Tool Chrome Extension

Despite the fact that Chrome's worked in spell checker can assist you to fix some spelling botches, it is worked to assist you with checking and fix syntactic mistakes. Language Tool will assist you with comprehending sentence structure mistakes in excess of 20 distinct dialects.

This tool chips away at a few sites both via web-based networking media and furthermore on email inboxes. Language Tool serves to underlines any content that needs adjustment and furthermore permits you to comprehend any syntactic mistake with only a tick. It assists with stamping in content with spelling botches and furthermore fix linguistic mistakes.

Grammarbase

Grammar Base is a free sentence structure checking tool that checks for everything from Accentuation to Style. It can assist you with fixing syntactic mistakes in your composition with only a single tick. It likewise checks your content against literary theft.

The best part about this syntax checker is that it is totally free and doesn't require any moves up to open more highlights. It deals with practically all sites including Gmail and Facebook.

Ginger

Ginger is one of the most well-known syntax checking tools on the Web. It permits you to fix sentence structure botches with only a tick. It likewise causes you to get recommendations for clearness and rethinking sentences.

With this tool, you can without much of a stretch interpret the content with a single tick. With the free form, you can fix practically all basic sentence structure botches in your composition and records over the web. This tool with Reddit, Facebook, Gmail, Google Docs, and practically even some different destinations.

Plagiarism Checkers

Prowritingaid

ProWritingAid is a free tool that checks your composition for sentence structure slip-ups and offers proposals to improve your composing style. It can assist you with forestalling missteps and make your composing more grounded. It additionally accompanies a written falsification checker.

It takes a shot at practically all sites over the web including email inboxes, Twitter, and other famous locales. It accompanies an implicit Thesaurus that offers proposals to improve your composition.

All the proposals can be applied with only a single tick directly from the content as this extension will feature the content consequently that needs revision or improvement.

Plagly

Plagly is a language checker and written falsification checker. It checks your content against a huge number of pages on the web and reports stealing entries in your content. It likewise offers proposals to fix language structure mistakes in your composition.

In spite of the fact that the initial hardly any activities are free; you have to pay a moderate month to month expense to get full access to the tool and boundless copyright infringement checking.

Mybib

MyBB is a free reference generator extension for Google Chrome. This chrome extension prompts you on whether a source is believable. It will assist you with generating references dependent on in excess of 9000 upheld, pre-characterized reference styles which incorporates APA, AMA, MLA, Harvard, and Chicago.

You can either duplicate your book reference to the clipboard or download it as a Word record. It can do what Easy Bib and Refer to This for Me improve. This is my suggested tool. CITE THIS FOR ME

Cite This for Me naturally makes site references and referencing in reports with a wide range of styles to look over. The styles incorporate Chicago, APA, MLA, and Harvard.

It does everything with only a tick of a catch. It permits you to make lovely references that look great and are adequate for scholarly use.

Easybib

Easy Bib is a free Chrome extension that refers to sites with a single tick and it additionally informs you of the validity concerning the sites you are referring to. It is vastly improved to depend on Easy Bib than a theory all alone.

It can inform you which references are acceptable and can be utilized and the one you ought to maintain a strategic distance from simply like a plague.

Google Dictionary

Google Dictionary Google's legitimate Chrome extension that permits you to see definitions straightforwardly from Google's authentic word reference. Not anymore looking through words on Google to check their significance or spelling.

You can either tap the chrome extension symbol and type/glue the word you need Google to characterize. Or then again, you can basically double-tap a word anyplace on the page and this extension will show you the significance in a little in-line popup box.

Power Thesaurus

Power Thesaurus is a free Chrome extension that can show you the antonyms and equivalents without leaving the page you found the word on. It can assist you with improving your composition by making it super-simple to discover comparable, all the more remarkable words to supplant your powerless words.

You can check the Thesaurus utilizing this extension by either choosing a word and right-tapping the choice. Or, on the other hand, you can tap the extension symbol in the menu bar to type the word physically and search the Thesaurus.

Quillbot

Quillbot is a free chrome extension that causes you to supplant words with their choices from the Thesaurus with only a tick. Rather than discovering options for each word all alone; you can essentially place a passage or sentence in this tool and snap the Plume it catches to create another section with elective words.

Stay Focused

In the event that you don't care for squandering hours via web-based networking media locales or even YouTube, at that point this application named 'Remain Centered' is the correct chrome extension you have been searching for. It helps square diverting sites by limiting 5-minute online networking registration which can transform into hours.

This extension permits you to set an everyday stipend limit for "internet-based life and diverting sites." It defaults to just 10 minutes. Your day by day remittance is the quantity of minutes you are permitted to peruse the locales in your interruption list.

On the off chance that you are a bad-to-the-bone profitability nerd; you can empower the atomic alternative from the settings which obstruct all the sites totally. The atomic choice can hinder all sites on the off chance that you need to invest energy disconnected dealing with troublesome stuff when you can't manage the cost of interruptions.

In the event that you need to peruse the Web openly on ends of the week or after work; you can modify the Dynamic Hours and Dynamic Days alternatives. You can enter all the locales you wish to obstruct in the interruptions list from the alternatives menu or you can tap the extension's symbol in the menu bar and add the present site to the rundown from that point.

Evernote Web Clipper

Evernote is the most mainstream note-taking application utilized by a large number of individuals around the globe. It can cause you increasingly beneficial as well as helps you to recall all that you learn. The best part about utilizing Evernote is the capacity to catch notes from online content, for example, website pages, messages, and other content with only a tick.

Evernote's note-taking procedure can accelerate your work process and offer a simple method to store all that you learn.

Evernote Web Scissors permits you to catch nearly everything on the Web. From inquire about material to images; you can save everything to your Evernote account with only a couple of snaps.

This extension additionally permits you to take screen captures. The best part about this extension is that it permits you to catch just pieces of a page. In addition, it can assist you with choosing the contents of website pages like Tweets, Reddit Posts, Blog Entries, and some more.

The great part for sparing content with the Internet Scissors is that you have a made sure about duplicate in your Evernote whether the page is on the web or has gone disconnected.

Todoist

Todoist is one of the most famous lineups for the day applications. It offers applications for all gadgets including Android, iOS, and so forth.

Keeping a lineup for the day in your mind will just injure your efficiency. The Todoist Chrome extension permits you to remain beneficial the entire day without overlooking any of your assignments. The spotless interface makes it simple to watch out for every one of your undertakings for the afternoon.

Todoist is made in light of coordinated effort. You can without much of a stretch work together with others who use Todoist on the undertakings and ventures. You can leave remarks on assignments for your schoolmates.

What I like the most about Todoist is that it naturally proposes you time and date for undertakings dependent on your calendar. At the point when you make an assignment, it will propose a date on the off chance that you click the calendar symbol close to the undertaking name.

To improve your work process, Todoist permits you to partition your errands with activities and marks. You can likewise make channels to channel errands dependent on needs, undertakings, and what their identity is allotted to. Todoist can be an insignificant plan for the day or an undeniable profitability machine with bunches of highlights, for example, Undertakings, Marks, Rehash, Updates, Channels, Names, and some more.

Dualless

Dualless encourages you to work with two open windows one next to the other. Taking a shot at only one screen can be tiring a direct result of all the exchanging between different windows. On the off chance that you can't manage the cost of two screens; you can utilize Dualless to mastermind two windows next to each other with only a couple of snaps.

You can relocate windows next to each other yourself however this extension encourages you to do it with only a couple of snaps. Dualless offers a wide range of design varieties to browse. You should simply choose two tabs you need to part and snap the extension's symbol to choose the window split design.

CHAPTER 11:

Tips and Tricks

Both teachers and students can benefit from Google Classroom. It is a secure platform that brings together some of the best apps that Google has to offer to help teachers get the most out of their lectures and students to learn in new and exciting ways. Here we will look at some of the tips and tricks that both students and teachers can try to get the most out of the Google Classroom platform.

Tips for Teachers

Tip 1: Learn all the ways to give feedback.

Your students are going to thrive with as much feedback as you can provide them, and the classroom offers you many options for this. You can leave comments on assignments that students hand in, on the file that is submitted, through email, and so much more. Consider the best places to leave feedback and let your students know so they can be on the lookout for ways to improve.

Some of the ways that you can utilize comments include:

- **Class comments**—you can do this by starting a common for the whole class on the outside of the assignment or in the announcement. It is going to be a comment that the entire course is going to see, so don't use it if you just want to talk to the individual student. It is an excellent option to use if you're going to answer a question that a lot of people have.

- **Private comments**—you can do this by going into the file of an individual student. You will be able to see the submissions this student has made and can click on the comment bar near the bottom. When you add a comment, the student will be the only one who can see it.

- **Comments to media**—you can do this by clicking on the file that the student submitted to you. Highlight the area and then comment on that particular part of the project. It can help you to show an example of the student or explain your thoughts and how something needs to be changed.

Tip 2: Use the description feature

When creating an assignment, make sure to add a nice long description. It is where you explain what the task is all about, how to complete it, and even when the assignment is due. Often students are juggling many classes all at once, and by the time they get to the task; they have forgotten all the instructions you gave them in class. Or if a student missed class that day; the description can help them understand what they missed. A good report can help to limit emails with questions and can help students get started on the assignment without confusion.

Tip 3: Reuse some of your old posts

At times, you may have an assignment, question, or announcement that is similar to something you have posted before. For example, if you have a weekly reading or assess task that is pretty much the same every week; you will be able to use the reuse option in the classroom. To do this, just click on the "+" button that is on the bottom right of the screen, and then you will then be able to select "Reuse post." Pick from a list of options that you already used for the class. If there are any modifications, such as a different due date, you can make those before posting again. When reusing the post, you have the option to create new copies of the attachments that were used in the original posting.

Tip 4: Share your links and resources

There may be times that you find a fascinating document, video, or other media that you would like your students to see. Or, they may need resources for an upcoming project, and you want to make it easier for them to find. In this case, you should use the announcement feature. It allows all the essential documents to be listed right at the top of the classroom rather than potentially getting lost further down in assignments.

It is a great tip to use for items of interest that you would like to share with your students or for documents and files that they will need right away. If you have a resource that the students will need throughout the year; you should place it into the "About" tab to prevent it from getting lost as the year goes on.

Tips for Students

Tip 1: Pick one email for all of your classes

Consider having a dedicated email that is for all of your classes. You don't need to separate it and have an email for each of your categories, but create a new email that will only accept information from all classes using Google Classroom. Whenever a teacher announces they use this platform; you will use this email. It helps you to keep all of your courses in one place and can prevent you from missing out on your announcements and assignments because they got lost in all your emails.

Tip 2: Check your classes daily

As the year goes on, your teacher will probably get into a routine of when they make posts and you can check the class at that time. But it is still a good idea to stay on top of a class and check it each day. You never know when you may forget about an assignment that is almost due or when the teacher will add a special announcement for the whole class. If you only check your levels on occasion; you could miss out on a lot of valuable information along the way. Check-in daily to stay up to date and to get everything in on time.

Tip 3: Look at the Calendar

One of the first places you should go when opening up to a class is the calendar. It is going to list everything necessary that is coming your way in the few months (updated as the teacher adds new announcements and assignments), so you can plan out your time. For some students, it is easier to get a grasp on the work when it is in tablet form rather than just looking at a date in the announcements. Use this as a planning tool and check it often to see if there is anything new to add to your schedule.

Tip 4: Ask questions for clarification

The classroom makes it easier for students to ask the questions they need before starting an assignment. In some classes, it can be hard to find time to ask a question. When twenty or more students are asking questions at the same time, or the teacher runs out of time and barely gets the assignment out before the bell, many students may leave the classroom without any clue how to begin on a task.

With the classroom, the students can ask any questions they have when it is convenient. If they have a question about an assignment; they can comment on the task or send an email. If they have a question about some feedback that is left for a test or essay; they can ask it right on the assignment. The classroom has opened up many options for talking to your teacher and getting your questions answered, so don't be shy and sit in the dark when you need clarification.

Tip 5: Learn about all the features of Google

Google has many great features that both students and teachers can take advantage, many people don't realize all of the different apps that are available on Google, and since these apps can be used together with the classroom and are free, it is essential to take advantage of as many as possible. Some of the best Google products that can help with learning include:

- **Gmail**—Gmail makes it easier for students and teachers to communicate about the class without sharing the information with other students.

- **Calendar**—students will be able to see at a glance when essential assignments, tests, and additional information occur in their class.

- **Drive**—Drive is a great place to put all tasks, questions, and other documents that are needed to keep up in class. Teachers can place learning materials and assignments inside for the student to see, and students can submit their jobs all in one place.

- **YouTube**—students are used to spending time on YouTube, and teachers can use this to their advantage to find educational videos for their class. Students can either look at links that the teacher provides or search for their videos.

- **Docs**—this program works similarly to Microsoft Word, but since it is free, it can be helpful for those students who don't already have Word at home. Students can write, edit, and make changes just like on regular documents and then submit them back to the teacher.

- **Google Earth/Maps**—explores the world around us with these two great features. Google Earth lets students learn more about the world by allowing them to look up different areas and see them from an actual satellite. Google Maps can help with Geography around the world, or students can even create their Maps with this program.

These are just a few of the different apps available with Google that can make a difference in the way that students learn. While not all of them will apply to every class, a good understanding of each can help the teacher pick the right one for their quality and helps the student learn as much as possible.

Tip 6: Don't forget about tests and quizzes

Sometimes, a teacher may give you a few days to complete a test at home if there isn't enough time to do everything in the classroom. It gives you a bit of freedom to study for longer and fit the test around your schedule, but when a check isn't due right away; it is sometimes easy to forget about it. Make sure to watch your calendar and set up announcements to remind yourself that a vital assignment or test is due.

The issue with forgetting about some of these things is that with the right add-ons, the system may grade the test as incomplete or give you zero (if the test is multiple choices). The teacher may be willing to go back in and fix the grade or extend the due date if you talk to them, but it is still better to just get the test done in the first place. It shows that you can adhere to deadlines and saves some time for your teacher.

Google Classroom may seem like a simple platform, but there is just so much that you can do with it both as a teacher and as a student. The options for learning, sending information back and forth, and all the organization and freedom now available in the classroom can make this an attractive choice for many schools.

CHAPTER 12:

FAQs about Google Classroom

As a teacher, there are a lot of different options that you can use to make the most out of your classroom and you may be curious as to why Google Classroom is the best option to help you out. There are many questions that you may have that pertain to Google Classroom. Some of the questions that you may have about Google Classroom include:

Is It Easy to Get Started with Google Classroom?

Yes, it is really easy to work with Google Classroom, but you do need to remember that it is necessary to have the Google Apps for Education and your domain needs to be verified.

How Are Apps for Education and Classroom Connected?

To keep things simple, Google Classroom is not able to work without the help of Google Apps for Education. While you are able to use the Apps for Education all on its own; you will find that using Google Classroom is going to help to make all of it organized and it is much easier to work with. With the help of both the Classroom and Apps working together, both the students and the teachers are able to access the spreadsheets, slideshows, and documents as well as other links without having to worry about attachments and more. Even giving and receiving assignments and grades are easier when these two are combined together. In addition, there is the option to download the Classroom Mobile app, which will make it easier to access your classes whenever and wherever you would like. This is going to be great for students who are on the go and don't have time to always look through their laptop to see announcements. Even teachers are able to use this mobile app to help them get up assignments and announcements when they are on the go so, they can concentrate on other tasks later on.

Does It Cost to Use Google Classroom?

One of the best things about using Google Classroom is that it is completely free. All you need is a bit of time to help get it all set up, but it will not include any out of pocket costs to make it work. You will have to wait about two weeks in the beginning for your application to be reviewed before you are able to use the class, so consider setting this up early to prevent issues with falling behind. You will never have to pay for anything when you are using Google Classroom. If you run into a vendor who is asking for you to pay for Google Classroom; you should report them to Google. It is highly likely that this is a fake vendor so do not work with them or provide them with any of your payment information. Google Classroom is, and always will be, free for you to use.

Can I Still Use Classroom If It Is Disabled on My Domain?

One of the nice things about working with Classroom is that even if it has been disabled on a certain domain, you are still able to use it. With that being said, there are going to be a few restrictions. While you may still be able to get access to a lot of the features, such as Google Drive, Google Docs, and Gmail; you may not be able to see some of the slides, docs, and sheets that were saved in the classroom. It is always best to have your domain turned on when you are working in Google Classroom because this ensures that you are able to use all of the features that are available through the Classroom.

Do I Need to Have Gmail Enabled to Use Classroom?

It is not necessary to have Gmail enabled in order to use the Google Classroom. You are able to use the Classroom as much as you would like without enabling Gmail, but you would find that you wouldn't be able to receive notifications if the Gmail account isn't turned on. If you would like to have some notifications sent to you, you need to have Gmail enabled.

If you are not that fond of using the Gmail account for this; it is possible to set up your own email server to make it work. This way, you will still be able to receive the notifications that are needed from the Classroom while using the email server that you like the most.

Will I Have to Work with Ads on Google Classroom?

Many people like to work with Google Classroom because they don't have to worry about seeing ads all over the place. The classroom was designed for educational purposes, and Google recognizes that people don't want to have to fight with ads all of the time when they are learning. You can rest assured that Google and Classroom are not going to take your information and use it for advertising. This is part of the privacy and security that is offered with Google Classroom, which will protect both the student and the teacher from any phishing or spam.

Yes, those with disabilities are able to use Google Classroom. Some of the features are not yet complete, but Google is working to make some improvements to the classroom so that those who have disabilities can use it too. Aside from using the Screen reader; there are a few other features that you can use with android including:

- **Braille Back:** this is a great feature that is going to allow for Braille to be displayed on the Android Device, as long as you have your Bluetooth installed. This is also going to work with the Screen Reader feature that we talked about before. With this feature, you will also be able to input your text while interacting with your Android device.

- **Switch Access:** it is also possible for you to use Switch Access, which is a tool that allows you to control your device with two or more switches. This is great for those who are dealing with limited mobility. It is also a good way to get notifications and alerts.

You are also able to tweak some of the settings that are in Google Classroom in regards to color correction, magnification, captions, touch and hold, using a speaking password, and more.

As you can see, there are a lot of neat things that you are able to do when it comes to using Google Classroom and it is pretty easy for everyone to be able to use. If you ever have some other questions about Google Classroom; you can always contact their support to get the assistance that you need.

CHAPTER 13:

Pros & Cons of Using Google Classroom

Pros

This platform has several features. Some are shown below:

- **Easy to use:** very easy to use. As M. Janzen said, "Google's classroom program is just a deliberate learning interface and options used to initiate and monitor activities; emails, notifications of relevance to the whole course or person, and gives notices of support."

- **Cloud-based:** Google Classroom offers increasingly sophisticated and valid innovations in the learning environment and Google applications are a series of important cloud-based business communication tools used by all professional staff.

- **Free:** there are no usage costs. Anyone with or without a Google Account can create and participate in lessons.

- **Compatible with mobile phones:** as M. Janzen said, "Today's educational environment requires access to

117

interesting and simple study materials." Google Classroom is designed to be responsive. Useful for use on any cell phone.

- **Save time:** Google Classroom saves students and teachers time. As Iftekhar said, "Coordinating with other Google applications such as presentations, documents, records, and spreadsheets. The whole process of evaluation, activities, reviews, formative evaluations, and feedback is divided and simplified."

Cons

Despite its many benefits, Google Classroom is limited. Such as:

- **Limited options:** Google Classroom is not synchronized with Google Calendar or other calendars. It is difficult for teachers to prescribe curricula and set deadlines for assignments.

- **About "goggles:"** Pappas describes Google Classroom as "goggles." This includes some buttons known to Google customers. In this case, people who see customers of Google articles for the first time (such as elementary and college students) can be confused or do more to learn these signs. Only Google Classroom coordinates YouTube to share videos. Other popular tools like SlideShare, Facebook, and others don't work in Google Classroom.

- **No mechanical updates:** Google Classroom does not automatically receive updates of streaming activities. Students must have the usual prerequisites, otherwise, clear notice is required.

- **Difficult to share with students:** it is not possible to share files with many classmates unless students become file owners. However, if you become the owner of the file, you must ask the teacher for permission to share the archive.

- **Change the problem:** after creating and distributing the project, students become owners of the archive. As owners, they have the right to change. In the long run, if desired, all parts of the project can be revoked, even if by chance by some students.

- **There are no automatic tests and quizzes:** Google Classroom does not compile computer-related exams and tests. Therefore, it cannot replace the other available learning management systems (LMS).

- **Impersonal:** still provides a mixed resume but is not compatible with other instant messenger programs such as Google Hangouts. In this case, Google Docs makes collaboration between students and teachers difficult. Basically, live chat is unlikely in Google Classroom; at least not yet.

Google Classification Teaching Quality

To monitor that Google Classroom affects listening skills; experts analyze the following search opportunities for research and make some recommendations.

This research is an operational research conducted by 40 scholars from Daffodil International University in Bangladesh. The Master is a first-year student with a degree in ordinary English. Scientists use quantitative research methods to gather information. The statistical analysis of relative percentages and student achievement levels was obtained from four different projects that had an impact on student skills. Experts found a lot of help from hearaminute.com in building search tools. This research was conducted with the permission of the university authorities.

To complete this study, Google Classroom researchers created a classroom called "Student Skills" and invited students to participate. Since students use Gmail accounts for a domain check (provided by the university), they can easily enter the classroom. The experts assigned four listening projects for the presentation for four consecutive weeks. Activities are a basic exercise to fill gaps and correct them together.

ELT experts point out that "listening skills" are one of the four language skills that are ignored, as they lack the ability and training to make positive use of the resources available to teach listening L2 students. This is conceived by students and teachers.

Students in Bangladesh tend to develop their English learning experience. However, today's young people are familiar with technology, which is an integrated resource for ELT professionals conducting research. This shows how Google Classroom can be used as a learning tool to improve students' listening skills. As a result, the positive impact of using Google Classroom on college lenders proves its worth.

Conclusion

Finally, the doubt on whether you are a beginner on Google Classroom is disappeared currently. The reality is that also the so-called "pro" would certainly doff their hats for you if you are able to sensibly make use of the text succinctly. If you doubt that, then find among them and exchange expertise and also see his/her comment on you. You have been taught on the benefits of Google Classroom, which undoubtedly was the first thing you learnt. The advantage is inexhaustible yet the significant ones are embedded below and also you can flaunt it is not a wild-goose chase to take on the use of Google Classroom.

Yet, you found out about just how to get going with Google Classroom, which is very important. Many stuck at the astonishing stage of concept regarding numerous inventions or technology or service since they lack understanding exactly how to get it began. You discovered the site link and also requires you require to keep the setting when starting using Google Classroom. Really it is a crucial aspect of it however not the main due to the fact that without more activities and knowledge concerning another other, you are like not beginning it.

After registration as well as being part of the elite neighborhood of teachers or trainees who await the future; you still relocated further to discover how to utilize Google Classroom. The action is necessary as you were shown on how to produce class, just how to structure it, how students can join your class, how to welcome therefore several others. These are crucial details you require to get familiarized with due to the fact that you will certainly use them each day you are instructing.

Likewise, applications that can be used in simplifying your ease of access and also for benefit were taught. There are a large number of applications with their unique attributes and contents that make making use of Google Classroom better on different tools. Some of the applications that were highlighted and also clarified are BookWidget, Duncee, Nearpod, and so on. These applications with various other good one's support using Google Classroom on your device at your convenient time. More so, student approach ideas were educated in the body of the text after the intro of the applications that can be utilized. These ideas are germane to efficient teaching on Google Classroom. You were taught how to email students whatever you want them to understand, how to make the statement, how to make use of the ideal comment you would give class, and more.

Making use of Google Classroom can be less complicated by adopting the best practices and methods for the tasks you want to carry out. Various best practices and also techniques were intimated to you in the body of the text. These were instructed to get the most out of the classroom, so you must endeavor to use it continually. Additionally, the functions offered on Google Classroom as well as devices that can be beneficially used. There are numerous features such as Assignments, Notifications, Comments, Google Forms, Google Schedule, etc. that you may be oblivion of unless you are taught. They make Google Classroom more interesting as they create an avenue for simpler teaching and learning at the same time. They collectively beautify the learning setting for both the teachers and the students. Detailed procedures of using them were found out in this text.

Using Google Classroom can be easier when the nitty-gritty of how to communicate with the trainee successfully is known. Therefore, a thorough description on how to communicate with the student using the Google Classroom was offered. The stipulation of that does not just make Google Classroom simpler however likewise streamlines the teaching and also removes the trouble several educators have while teaching in physical class. Afterward, a much more detailed explanation on how to prepare the assignment, grade it as well as announcements were provided to you. On top of that, much like the traditional physical class; you would need to return the task given in order to grade it and record, so a method to accomplish that on Google Classroom was given. The intriguing component is that; all works can be collected from all the students on the same web page.

Making use of modern technology such as the Google Classroom in order to obtain the commitment of trainees was shown. The primary reason behind adopting the brand-new approach and also attempting new things such as the use of Google Classroom is to acquire the academic objective.

The attainment of the objective hinges on the students' commitment, so the demand for it. Nonetheless, ideal practices that can be embraced in the Google Classroom were brought to you. The need for it is clear just as you need a mentor to look forward to in anything you intend to do well.

Lastly, how to improve your teaching by making use of Google Classroom was discovered. There are various methods to do that, some of the instructed ones are using partnership/collaboration, keeping tab of activities, use of Google calendar judiciously, integrating of Google Forms, Google Drive, Google Sites, Google Maps, and various other services such as YouTube within the Google Classroom.

Now I believed you must have been attempting everything you found out until now on Google Classroom, nevertheless, if you have not, why not start now. Now that you have all the tools required, take your tool, and also start using them.

Printed in Great Britain
by Amazon

63044018R00077